The Nottingham Lots

The Nottingham Lots

A Tercentenary Celebration 2001

East Nottingham Trustees

Library of Congress Number:		2005909543
ISBN:	Hardcover	1-4257-0044-6
	Softcover	1-4257-0043-8

This book was printed in the United States of America.

To order additional copies of this book, contact:
Xlibris Corporation
1-888-795-4274
www.Xlibris.com
Orders@Xlibris.com

26254

Contents

In loving memory of

Ron Stroud (1955-2003)

and

Erasmo “Gene” Galantino (1929-2004)

Nottingham Lots Tercentenary

Celebrated Saturday and Sunday,
September 29 & 30, 2001 on the grounds of the
Brick Meetinghouse
Calvert, Maryland
Cecil County

This 300-year celebration was prepared by:

The Nottingham Lots Tercentenary Committee

Billie Anne Bradley, Oxford, PA
Anne Coplev. Landenberg, PA
Lowell Haines. Rising Sun, MD
Suzanne Lamborn, Nottingham, PA
Jon Magoon, Oxford, PA
Geraldine McKeown, Elkton, MD
Edward Plumstead, Rising Sun, MD
Paul Rodebaugh, West Chester, PA
Ronald E. Stroud, Oxford, PA

Martin Bradley, Oxford, PA
Robert Day, Dublin, MD
Charles Hilaman, Nottingham, PA
Harriet Magoon, Oxford, PA
James Matsen, Lincoln Univ., PA
Gail Pietrzyk, Oxford, PA
Miriam Reisler, Oxford, PA
Lee Stanton, Oxford, PA
Leonard Wilson, Elkton, MD

James Yerkes, Rising Sun, MD

We wish to especially acknowledge
Edward Plumstead
for his years of devoted study and care
centering on the
Brick Meetinghouse
and the Nottingham Lots.

Events

Saturday, 9/29/01

11:00 a.m. Students from George Fox Friends School perform the play, "The Penn Oak," written and directed by their Head of School, Linda Uberseder.

1:00 p.m. Robert W. Day, descendant of John and Lydia Ross Daye, speaks on the establishment of the Nottingham Lots and the early resident families.

2:00 p.m. Eric Chandlee Wilson, descendant of famous clock maker Benjamin Chandlee, tells of clock making in Calvert.

3:00 p.m. Paul Rodebaugh, Vice Chairman of the West Chester Historic and Architecture Review Board, treats John Churchman's Journal.

Sunday, 9/30/01

11:00 a.m. Friends meeting for worship.

Noon Covered dish (pot luck) luncheon in the yard. Please bring a favorite dish to share. If you prefer not to use single-service tableware, you may need to bring your own plates, cups, and implements.

1:00 p.m. Peace Pole dedication. More than 200,000 Peace Poles have been dedicated in 180 countries around the world. Their purpose is to spread the message, "May Peace Prevail on Earth," and to act as a constant reminder for us to visualize and pray for world peace.

1:30 p.m. Thom Jeavons, General Secretary of Philadelphia Yearly Meeting, speaks on modern Quaker faith and practice.

Activities & Exhibits

In addition to featuring knowledgeable speakers, Saturday will be full of activities and exhibits.

Throughout the day, ox-cart rides will be provided by John Williams, of Fruitland, Maryland. There will be a performance of a children's stage play, *The Penn Oak,* actually under our Penn Oak, between the meetinghouse and the food vendors.

A little farther away from the meetinghouse, you'll find various exhibitions of craftsmanship and displays of historical interest, in-cluding quilts, a potter's wheel, a blacksmith, and a wood turner. In this area, Geraldine McKeown will have for display and sale prints of her pertinent work, "Quaker Heritage."

Moving closer again towards the meetinghouse lawn, you'll come to the registration table. Our commemorative plates and tee-shirts may be purchased here. Please also browse the books we have on consignment from Per-idle Hill, the Quaker retreat center in Wallingford, PA.

Those who came hoping to share genealogical information may find each other at the tent nearest the cemetery. In that tent also are illustrations of the Nottingham Lots and related histories.

On Sunday, please join us for worship at 11:00. Then, after lunch, we'll dedicate a Peace Pole, and hear from Philadelphia Yearly Meeting's General Secretary Thom Jeavons.

Acknowledgements

This celebration is conducted by the East Nottingham Trust-ees, caretakers of the Brick Meetinghouse at Calvert, MD. The sale of tee-shirts and commemorative plates is intended to cover our costs

We would like to thank Union Fire Company No. 1 from Ox-ford, PA, whose auxiliary is selling lunch on Saturday. Please enjoy their cooking and thus support their long-standing volunteer organization. Desserts and snacks have been donated by Herr's Potato Chip Co. and George Fox Friends School

We are grateful to the Rising Sun Fire Police for traffic control, and the Cecil County Historical Society has helped us immeasurably

Thanks to all the individuals, churches and Friends Meeting community businesses and organizations who supported and helped to promote this event.

In celebration of the 300th anniversary of the Nottingham Lots settlement, that is now part of Cecil County, Maryland, we remember those pioneers who journeyed westward into the wilderness led by William Penn in the Spring of 1701.

Thirty-seven lots of about 500 acres were surveyed and the new owners drew lots for the tracts. Settlement and clearing the land be-gan in 1702. Tradition holds that William Brown was the first to take his axe in hand and strike it into a tree with the prayer, "In humble trust, we begin our labor."

On purchasing the lots, settlers paid eight British pounds for each 100 acres; additionally, they were to pay one shilling or two bushels of good wheat yearly in quitrent.

Andrew Job had been a sheriff in Chester County and con-vinced other settlers to come to the area. Many did, from around Chichester, including these, mentioned in Quaker minute books and other documents: Joel Baily, John Beales, Edward Beeson, John Churchman, James Cooper, Robert Dutton, Ebenezer Empson, John Guest. Randal Janney, Samuel Littler, Henry Reynolds, and John Richardson. Some of these families had started in New Jersey, but were enticed to this area by the tall timber of fine oak indicating that this was good farmland.

The great white oak tree near the meetinghouse, the emblem of our celebration, has been ring-dated to c. 1661.

The Brick Meetinghouse itself, now under the care of Nottingham Monthly Meeting in Oxford, PA, was built in 1724 on the land given by Penn to Quaker settlers back in 1701.

In 1748, that first meetinghouse burned and was rebuilt with a stone addition. In 1810 there was another fire. Quaker meeting minutes of that time report that a single poplar tree furnished the wood for all the benches inside the meetinghouse.

Worship, of course, is the primary use of the Brick Meetinghouse. However, over the years it has served other purposes. In 1762, a coeducational school for the poor of the area, including the local Negroes, was established. By this time, most Friends had agreed that slavery was wrong, even though few that continued to hold slaves needed to be censured by their meetings. During the Revolutionary War, the meetinghouse was used as a hospital, and the grounds were a camp for Lafayette on his way to Yorktown, Virginia.

The Tercentenary

The trustees of the East Nottingham Meetinghouse (Brick Meetinghouse) became aware that the origins of this meeting dated to 1701. This ancient meetinghouse located in Calvert, Maryland, and under the care of Nottingham Monthly Meeting of the Religious Society of Friends, is no longer regularly used for Quaker worship. The Nottingham Monthly Meeting in nearby Oxford, Pennsylvania directed the "Brick Trustees" to plan and execute an event to commemorate this impending 300-year anniversary.

The committee wished to recognize and honor the Quaker families who came to Nottingham 300 years ago. We felt they established an important community and made worthy contributions to humankind. Most notable was the pioneer, John Churchman, son of emigrants, who traveled and shared his religious beliefs and represented Friends to the wider world of the American colonies. He was not alone and most of the other families in the settlement were equally essential as they built the strong religious community in the Nottingham Lots and surrounding areas. The focus of this early community was the forty acres designated by William Penn to be a place of worship and burial for Friends. They labored mightily to build and maintain this Brick Meetinghouse, which later became the village name. It's quite remarkable that one tree which has been dated to the 1660's has watched over Friends as they continued the meetings at the Brick through the centuries. The committee also decided early to recognize and honor Mr. Edward Plumstead. We learned of his steady efforts for over fifty years to perpetuate the architectural integrity of this early settlement and its meetinghouses in Cecil County, Maryland. We experienced firsthand his extensive knowledge of the community. The stories he tells are captivating and have been captured for the future generations on audio and video recordings.

An initial meeting of the committee was held on Tuesday evening, July 18th, 2000 at the Brick Meetinghouse with thirteen present including a small kangaroo friend, Sarah, from the nearby Plumpton Park Zoo, accompanied by her master, Edward Plumstead. A second meeting was convened on Thursday, the 31st of August 2000 at the Brick and it was decided to host a two-day event to celebrate the 300-year anniversary in 2001. The work and success of this tireless committee was spurred along by an additional ten Monday evening meetings that extended from October 2000 to September 2001. Meetings were convened at the Brick, at Plumpton Park Museum, and Oxford Friends Meetinghouse. Attendance was steady and the committee comprised a select group of interested and talented individuals. These precious talents came together on Saturday and Sunday, September 29th and 30th, 2001.

We are particularly thankful to have enjoyed the keen experienced mind of Paul Rodebaugh, of West Chester, to suggest a framework for the celebration. Ron Stroud, of Oxford, contributed an essential service by providing the writing and publishing skills to produce the beautiful event brochures and the event program. Edward Plumstead, of Calvert, provided the skillful artwork that evolved into 150 beautiful commemorative plates and tee shirts. The committee bestowed plate number 1 of 150 to Edward. Gail Pietrzyk, also of Oxford, contributed enormously from her archival skills to produce the historical panels that enabled guests to examine the time line of the Nottingham Lots. Robert W. Day, of Moore, South Carolina, a descendent of one early Nottingham family, shared his academic skills and genuine interest in the topic to lead the series of Saturday afternoon speakers that drew guests to an overflowing meetinghouse. Suzanne Lamborn, Charles Hilaman, Lowell Haines, Lee Stanton, Billie Anne Bradley, James Matsen, and Robert Day, of Dublin, Maryland, are notable for their efforts to secure the facilities, exhibitors, and the numerous resources that enabled the weekend to be such an outstanding success.

The glow from this venture was an inspiration for the Oxford Friends Meeting that supported the committee throughout the year leading up to September 29th and 30th of 2001. The weather for the weekend was chilly and breezy with morning showers on Saturday. The sun returned for most of Saturday afternoon, which warmed the guests, who numbered up towards 500. A book was made available for guests to register their names and addresses. The exhibitors included Erasmo Galantino who demonstrated his skills as a potter. John A. Styer demonstrated woodcarving, and Alphonsus M.M. Moolenschot, a blacksmith, exhibited his craft. Watercolorist, Geraldine McKeown, released lithographic prints of her beautiful study of the Brick Meetinghouse, "Quaker Heritage" as part of the celebration. John Williams, of Fruitland, Maryland, provided ox cart rides to eager children. The children from the George Fox Friends School presented a play, "The Penn Oak."

Sunday morning before meeting for worship, the guests were able to admire a newly planted "Peace Pole" nearby to the meetinghouse. It expressed a message dear to all Friends of "May Peace Prevail on Earth" in four languages.

Finally, the reward to the committee was to observe people from far and wide enjoying a precious weekend of remembrance.

Martin Bradley, *event coordinator.*

Peace Pole dedicated on Sunday, September 30, 2001. More than 200,000 Peace Poles have been dedicated in 180 countries around the world. Their purpose is to spread the message, "May Peace Prevail on Earth," and to act as a constant reminder for us to visualize and pray for world peace. *Photo by Ronald E. Stroud*

Thom Jeavons, General Secretary of Philadelphia Yearly Meeting, speaks on modern Quaker faith and practice. *Photo by Ronald E. Stroud* Eric

Chandlee Wilson with Chandlee clock. *Photo courtesy Edward Plumstead.*

William Penn portrayed by David Rose with speaker, Paul Rodebaugh.
Photo by Ronald E. Stroud

Below: Students from George Fox Friends School perform the play, "The Penn Oak," written and directed by their Head of School, Linda Uberseder. *Photo by Ronald E. Stroud*

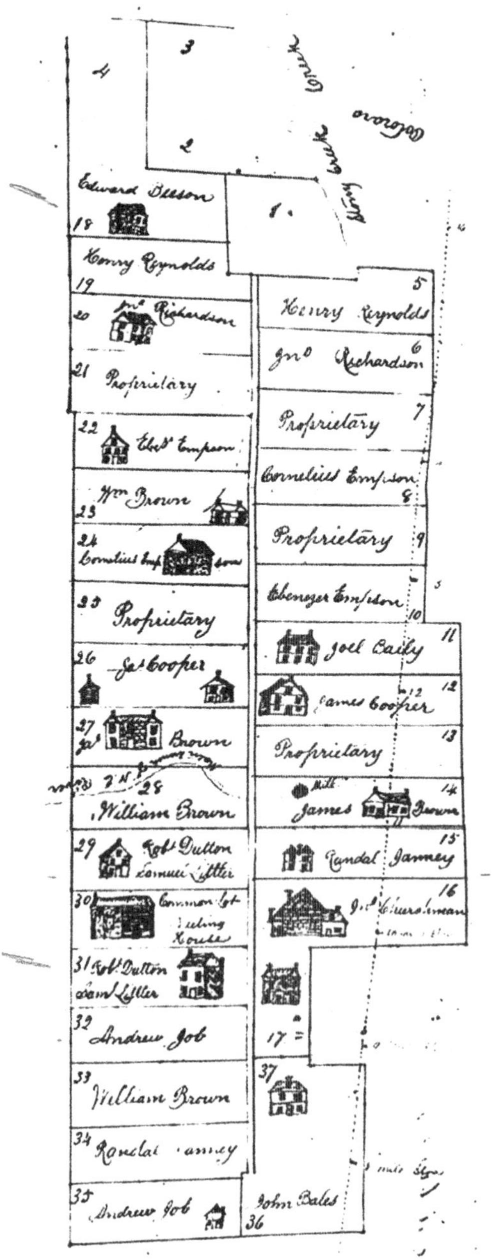

A draught of Nottingham Township, 1702.
From copy at Chester County Historical Society.

The Nottingham Lots and the Early Quaker Families

A Paper Presented by
Robert Warwick Day, Ph.D.
Spartanburg, South Carolina

September 29, 2001
East Nottingham Monthly Meeting
Calvert, Cecil County, Maryland

In celebration of the 300th anniversary of the founding in 1701 of the Nottingham Lots by William Penn and early Quaker settlers of Chester County, PA.

Good afternoon. Thank you so much for inviting me to be part of your program. I'd like to commend the outstanding work of the Oxford, PA Friends for planning and organizing this very special tercentenary anniversary celebration of the Nottingham Lots. Over a year's planning and many volunteer hours have gone into carrying out this special historical event. Congratulations to the members of the planning committee and to the many volunteers who had a role.

This weekend, you are part of a growing American pastime called "cultural history," in which people seek to learn more about how their ancestors lived and what happened in their lifetimes. Cultural history is now a reason for the growth of travel and tourism in America. I commend you for being here today whether you've come from across the road or from across the country to learn more about the origins of this wonderful area.

I have visited here at least six times over the past 25 years in undertaking my family genealogy. However, before preparing this talk, I decided to review Cecil County websites to see what local people are talking about and find out what's on their minds.

I discovered on a county chat room this spring a very profound entry in which a resident stated that "the past is what actually happened; history is only what the officials wrote down." There's probably much truth in this observation.

I've been asked to speak today on the historic founding of the Nottingham Lots and the early families that settled this area 300 years ago. I'd like to share today how the establishment of this area was motivated by a combination of land acquisition, religion and politics.

The history of the Nottingham Lots has been told and published at different times by historians, genealogists, Quakers, and families. Over these past 300 years, there has probably been both much fact and, yes, some folklore in describing what actually occurred on this historic land.

What I'd like to do this afternoon is use my interpretation of historical sources to describe the forces which gave rise to this area. I'll touch on the founding of this historic Quaker meetinghouse called East Nottingham Monthly Meeting, also known as The Brick Meetinghouse or "The Brick." Then, I'll also address the families and culture of the early Quaker families that settled Nottingham Lots. I may take a few liberties in interpreting certain events, but I'll attempt to be as historically accurate as possible. And please forgive me if I continue to perpetuate folklore after 300 years.

Lest we forget, this comer of Maryland was mostly part of southwestern Chester County, PA, one of William Penn's original counties after his founding of Pennsylvania in 1682. This area of the county represented the western frontier of Pennsylvania at that time, and the lands west of here were primarily tribal and unsettled by Europeans.

Native Americans, particularly descendants of the Susquehannocks and other tribes that had been displaced by the growth of colonizing settlers, once used the heavily forested lands here for their hunting and fishing grounds. William Penn's several treaties with the Indians, including one in 1705, probably helped minimize major outbreaks between the Colonists and the Native Americans living here.

Historically, the Nottingham Lots were "ground zero" for a multigenerational land dispute between the several Lords Baltimore and William Penn, his sons and grandsons over border rights. Unlike other English colonies in America, both Maryland and Pennsylvania were originally grants or gifts to Lord Baltimore and William Penn, respectively. Each had autonomy in governing his colony without the direct control of the English government.

It is apparent from the records that Maryland had its toehold in this area before Pennsylvania. The Maryland Charter of 1632 placed that colony's northern boundary near 40 degrees latitude, closer to Philadelphia. However, this border was never firmly established.

Fifty (50) years later, in 1682, William Penn received a grant of land from James 11 of England on the west side of the Delaware River and Delaware Bay. Penn appointed his cousin, William Markham, governor of Pennsylvania and appointed three commissioners to lay out the city of

Philadelphia. Penn continued to amass great land holdings in the new colony, as he had in England.

The primary dispute was over Lord Baltimore's claim to the northern border of Maryland and William Penn's claim to the southern border of Pennsylvania. This land dispute continued for another fifty years after Penn's death in 1718. It was not until the late 1760s that the boundary was drawn through the work of two eminent English mathematicians and astronomers, Charles Mason and Jeremiah Dixon.

The Nottingham Lots grew out of William Penn's tenacity in establishing his border rights. The second Lord Baltimore, Cecil Calvert, became more preoccupied with settling his border rights with the colony of Virginia to the south. At the same time, Penn was successful in attracting Quaker families primarily from the Philadelphia area and West Jersey as a means of fortifying his title to it.

In addition to the political differences between Lord Baltimore and William Penn, there were also differences in their religious backgrounds. Maryland was a Catholic-friendly colony and the Calverts were Catholic. There were strongly held feelings between them and the Protestant King William and Queen Mary of England. The late 1600s and early 1700s represented a turbulent time in the religious history of England. Lord Baltimore could not assume an adversarial role toward William Penn due to Lord Baltimore's complex relationships with the Crown of England at that time.

In the late 1600's, the second Lord Baltimore, Cecil Calvert, had a relative named George Talbot. Talbot, an Irishman who became Surveyor General of Maryland, was granted a patent for a huge tract of land of 32,000 acres known as the Susquehanna Manor to help settle English and Irish immigrants in Maryland. Talbot was an adventurous man who became embroiled in. a series of turbulent events, including a murder that resulted in his forfeiture of the Manor. William Penn used his dominant position to carve out over half of the former Susquehanna Manor for the new Nottingham settlement at the turn of the century.

In 1701, William Penn granted a warrant for 18,000 acres for the Nottingham Lots as one tract. The lots extended east to west about 1.0 mile across, from the present-day town of Rising Sun to the west to about 2 1/2 miles to the east of Brick Meetinghouse. The lots extended north to south at a maximum width of 3 miles.

In 1701, all 18,000 acres lay in Chester County, PA. However, after the settlement of the Mason-Dixon Line in the late 1,760's, only 1,300 acres of the original Nottingham Lots remained in Chester County and the other 16,700 acres became part of Cecil County, Maryland.

Penn's original tract was divided into lots running north and south, resulting in 37 lots. Each lot averaged approximately 500 acres and each was numbered between 1 and 37. It is generally believed that prospective owners made selections by the drawing of lots—hence, the use of the term "Lots."

The name "Nottingham" most likely came from William Penn's home in Nottinghamshire, England. The local township became known as East Nottingham and the meetinghouse became East Nottingham. Quakers and Scots-Irish Presbyterians settled the area to the west, known as West Nottingham.

According to the Pennsylvania Commissions of Property in 1701, the original families interested in purchasing one or more of the Nottingham Lots were to pay "8 pounds for every 100 acres within one year of date hereof, and one shilling for a yearly quitrent, for every 100 acres forever after, or in case of nonpayment, that they shall hold the land under the yearly rent of 2 bushels of good winter wheat for every 100 acres . . ."

So this became the purchase price and quitrent per 100 acres for each of the original owners. The average landowner of 500 acres of land would have paid 40 pounds sterling for his property at that time (or about $65 at the current exchange rate).

Subsequent to the establishment of the area, the Friends laid out a road through the center of the Nottingham Lots. This road was a continuation of the old road from Philadelphia to Darby, Chester, Kennett Square, New London, and then Nottingham. This was also the major road for Quaker migration from Philadelphia to the southwest, as a number of Quaker villages sprung up along this route in the late 1600s.

The Nottingham area at that time has been described as rich in natural resources, with heavily forested lands and trees that included hickory, chestnut, walnut, and oak. The land was fertile and the streams were said to be clear and vibrant. New economic opportunities were plentiful for new settlers to this area.

It is believed that two pioneer brothers, James and William Brown, both Quaker ministers, were among the first settlers here. They were sons of Richard and Mary Brown, members of Wellingborough Monthly Meeting in Northamptonshire, England, and apparently had become Friends before they came to America. Tradition has it that the Brown brothers were likely accompanied by several other founding members, including Andrew Job, John Churchman, and Henry Reynolds.

It is said that William Penn accompanied the Brown brothers and others to the area in 1701. On their last day, Penn is believed to have set apart and dedicated 40 acres of land, which is the land that we stand on today. Penn is quoted as saying that this land is "to them and their successors forever, for the combined purpose of public worship, the right of burial, and the privilege of education."

Over the next 50 years, all of these purposes were fulfilled with the establishment of the Meetinghouse, the burial yard, and a Quaker grade school which followed.

Several historical sources, however, imply that William Penn may not have been present at the surveying of the Lots. Penn had experienced financial setbacks both in Pennsylvania and England and was busy straightening out his financial affairs. Penn had returned from England in November 1699, after a long absence from the colony. He spent much of his time at his home in Pennsbury on the Delaware River and at his home in Philadelphia. Penn returned to England in October 1701, only to return to America very briefly between 1701 and his death in 1718.

It is possible that Penn left his agent James Logan of Philadelphia in charge of many of the proprietary affairs of Pennsylvania, including the surveying of and founding of the Nottingham Lots. Logan was the Secretary of the Pennsylvania Land Office, which represented William Penn's extensive land holdings. Penn had become overextended in his landholdings and financial obligations in both America and England and no doubt was distracted by these difficulties. It is conceivable that he was preparing to return to England, as he did in October 1701, and that he never came to Nottingham.

Whether Penn was present or not, however, he undoubtedly approved this location for the settlement. It is believed that his verbal declaration, made in 1701, was for 64 years the only title by which Friends held ownership of the land of the Brick Meetinghouse. In 1765, John and Thomas Penn, heirs of William Penn, made a deed to the Nottingham Quakers that gave them final title of ownership.

Nottingham was a frontier village for its first 30 years, while settlers cleared the land and built roads, shops, dwellings, and the Meetinghouse. The Lots were populated by "simple, frugal, and industrious people" who combined farming with one or more of the occupations of that time including milling, blacksmithing, carpentry, clock making, tanning. They raised extensive crops of wheat, corn, and vegetables. Tobacco was not grown here since the soil would not support it.

The community became highly self-sufficient by the sharing of services, such as home-building, relying very little on outside resources other than perhaps support from the Philadelphia Yearly Meeting of Friends.

The religious and cultural heart of the Nottingham Lots was clearly the East Nottingham Monthly Meeting (or Brick Meetinghouse), which was part of William Penn's original plan. In either 1707 or 1709, a log cabin was built to serve as the first Nottingham Meetinghouse. In 1715, the East Nottingham Monthly Meeting was organizationally affiliated with the Newark Monthly

Meeting. In 1718, Brick Meetinghouse was put under the care of New Garden Monthly Meeting after New Garden separated from Newark.

In 1724, the 2 1/2 story structure was built and in 1730, the East Nottingham Monthly Meeting (or Brick Meetinghouse) was organized as a separate Monthly Meeting. There were two separate sides, one of brick and one of stone, one side for the men and the other side for the women. It is thought to have been the largest Quaker meetinghouse south of Philadelphia, within the Philadelphia Yearly Meeting, for the next few decades.

The social traditions of the early Nottingham founders were closely aligned to their conservative religious beliefs. The Friends addressed themselves as "thee" and "thou." They dressed very conservatively and were simple in their daily lives. Their household possessions were few, but land ownership appeared to be a high priority.

They were also very human, according to meeting records. Some Friends were "disowned" from Quaker meetings for a variety of reasons, including marrying out of unity, excessive drinking, fornication, taking an oath, assaulting another person, and others. The Quaker faith and moral conscience in this small community was apparently strong, conservative, and rigid.

The role of Quaker women was quite broad, as they frequently became the "spiritual force" of the community and assumed significant roles in managing the affairs of the women's Quaker meetings and caring for neighbors in need. Quaker women were known for their revolutionary child rearing practices, which were considered advanced for the times. Women also pursued other household tasks such as candle making, gardening, and the making of clothing.

Children were very much a part of the family work unit, as their roles were defined by religious tenets. The Nottingham Quakers apparently supported a basic education. A Friends school built of logs was erected here about 1730 and served the community for the next 65 years. It reflected their basic religious beliefs about education and learning. Education much beyond the elementary level was virtually unknown and unavailable, since Friends viewed advanced formal education with suspicion for many years.

The first homes in the village, called "bee hives," were very small, stone houses built on two levels. As wealth amassed in the community by the 1730s, somewhat larger, but modest, four-room houses of brick and/or stone were built. They often had a "keeping room" with a cooking fireplace and had very simple, narrow staircases to the second floor. They were occasionally built with the help of neighboring Friends. To this day, several homes built in the 1700s, such as the Messer Brown home, have the names of the builders inscribed in the exterior brick.

One of the greatest challenges the Nottingham Lots landowners and their descendants confronted was gaining title to their property after the death of

William Penn in 1718. This particularly caused difficulty when property was to be resold to subsequent purchasers and the lots were subdivided.

Another challenge was that many Nottingham landowners apparently failed to pay their quitrents, since for years, it was uncertain whether they were to be paid to Philadelphia or to Annapolis. So many landowners just didn't pay at all.

The Nottingham Quakers were very traditional about their rites of burial. The graveyard partially surrounded the Meetinghouse. Initially, there were no grave markers or stones to identify the deceased. Later, there were small stones used with no markings, and then subsequently, small stones with inscriptions were added. The larger headstones were a later addition and seemed to be out of form with Quaker simplicity.

The geographical identity of the Nottingham Lots had always been somewhat confusing. The people seemed to have very strong alliances to Pennsylvania and Delaware. The name "Nottingham Lots" appeared on the early surveys and maps. The town name of "Brick Meetinghouse" appears on Maryland maps of the 1800's. The town was renamed "Calvert" about 1880, since the postal service felt the name of Brick Meetinghouse was too long. "Nottingham" became the name of the relocated town now several miles north of here in Chester County on US Highway # 1.

The original Nottingham Lots were settled by 15 families, some of whom held more than one lot. Five owners never lived on their land here but were instead, absentee owners who lived mostly in the Philadelphia area. William Penn apparently retained 3,000 acres for his personal use, known as the "proprietary lots."

The original purchasers of lots included the following individuals: Joel Baily, John Bales or Beals, Edward Beeson, James Brown, William Brown, John Churchman, James Cooper, Robert Dutton, Cornelious Empson, Ebeneser Empson, Randal Janney, Andrew Job, Samuel Littler, Henry Reynolds, and John Richardson.

A review of genealogical records reveals that most of these first purchasers were middle-class yeomen born in England during the middle 1600's and died in the Nottingham area in the early 1700's. Their roots were mostly in the northern England counties of Cheshire, Durham, Lancashire, and Yorkshire, although some other English counties were represented.

Nearly all of the original Nottingham families came from within a 50-mile radius of Philadelphia before settling here. All were Quakers, and most of them transferred their certificate of membership from other Quaker meetings to the Brick Meetinghouse after its establishment. It can be surmised that William Penn or his agents knew at least some of the families in England or Pennsylvania and encouraged them to relocate to Nottingham.

Among the original owners, certainly the Brown brothers (James and William) represented the strong religious values of the community. They are believed to have held the first Quaker meetings in their homes about 1704 prior to the building of the Meetinghouse. By 175 1, six members of the Brown family, four men and two women, were ministers here in Nottingham.

Andrew Job was a carpenter and the sheriff of Chester County between 1697 and 1701. He along with John Churchman and their families were first to present certificates of transfer from the Chester Monthly Meeting to East Nottingham Monthly Meeting in 1706.

Andrew Job also established the historic Blue Ball Tavern on Lot 35 of the Nottingham Lots in about 1710. This roadside tavern provided shelter for travelers for the next 100 years. Andrew Job was apparently a close friend of William Penn and was influential in attracting new families to the Nottingham Lots.

John Churchman came to Nottingham with his parents about 1705 and became a minister. He was legendary for his religious travels throughout the colonies, Great Britain and Europe and kept a journal that was later published. He also became quite wealthy and built a home which was almost considered pretentious for this small Quaker village.

The Nottingham Friends were also visited occasionally by traveling male and female Quaker ministers from other parts. Many were on their way by horseback to other parts of Maryland, Virginia, and the Carolinas to spread the faith to relocated families. Local families here would take the traveling missionaries into their homes for the night. The connections between the Friends in PA, MD, VA and the Carolinas were strong through the 1700's, as Quaker ministers and missionaries traveled about the colonies.

After about 1710, there were other Quakers who came to the Nottingham Lots in search of land and a new life. Most of this second wave of settlers had their early roots throughout England, Ireland, Scotland and Wales.

One of the more prominent families in this second wave was the England family. England's have lived in this area until the present time, and a nearby road in the village is named for this historic family. Other prominent families that came very early were the families of Chandlee, Coppock, Gatchell, Haines, Hollingsworth, Kirk, Preston, Pugh, Sidwell, White, and Wright.

All told, there were more than 70 family surnames represented in the early records of Brick Meetinghouse. Many of these settlers and their descendants intermarried with neighboring families and many were married in Brick Meetinghouse.

It's important to know that the original Quaker families of the Nottingham Lots were virtually a self-contained community and separate from other religious and ethnic groups in the region. Welsh Baptists had settled the Welsh

Tract to the north. Scots-Irish Presbyterians had settled in western Cecil County and York County, PA. German Reformed and Lutherans had settled to the northwest in Lancaster and northern York Counties in Pennsylvania.

The Tidewater area of southern Cecil County in the late 1600s and early 1700s was a curious combination of two religious groups. Early Quaker families who had escaped religious persecution in Virginia lived amongst the Church of England loyalist planters who grew tobacco and supported a slave-based economy.

The early Nottingham Quakers were set apart from these other groups, both geographically and socially, but apparently were on good terms with them.

After 1730, some of the Nottingham descendants began to move to other regions. Cheaper land prices, better economic opportunities, plus overcrowding caused by the influx of settlers who had purchased land near Nottingham, were factors that caused some of the descendant families to migrate south and west.

Some of these families moved to Prince George's County, MD, Northern Virginia, the Shenandoah Valley, central and southside Virginia, the central Carolinas and Georgia. They were among the first generation of pioneer families of the uplands region of the South. Hopewell Monthly Meeting near Winchester, VA, for example, had a good representation of Nottingham Friends who followed Alexander Ross to the Shenandoah Valley to settle 100,000 acres in the 1730s.

This migration to the South continued until late in the 18th century. The Friends followed a similar migratory path down the Valley of Virginia as the Scots-Irish and Germans of Pennsylvania.

However, for many of the Friends, who were accustomed to religious freedom in Pennsylvania, the issues of religious persecution and slavery arose in these new lands and were foreign to their beliefs. Some affluent Quakers in both Pennsylvania and the South were slave owners themselves but were often admonished by their own members.

The western lands in Kentucky, Ohio, Indiana, and western Pennsylvania were opened up to settlers after 1790. Some Nottingham Quakers and southern Quakers with early roots in Nottingham saw fit to relocate their families to the west to pursue new economic opportunities.

Quaker migration in the 19th and 20th century continued all the way to the West Coast and to Canada. The path of migration through the mid-western states of Ohio, Indiana, Illinois, and Iowa and on to the West Coast was particularly common between 1800 and 1890. Another common migratory path was from Alabama to Texas and westward. Some of the early Anglo-American settlers in Southern California in the 1880s were Friends descended from Nottingham.

And then, of course, there are many descendants of the early Nottingham families who remained in this area or relocated to the Philadelphia or Baltimore areas and intermarried and raised their families. Migration to these nearby urban areas accelerated through the last century, as employment and educational opportunities attracted large numbers of area youth.

. . . which brings us up to present times . . .

Some of you here today, whether you know it or not, are descendants of one or more of the original Nottingham families. Nearly 12 generations later, some of you live very close to your Nottingham roots.

Many of us here today share a common early experience that has allowed us to share a common thread of history. Three hundred years later, Nottingham Quaker descendants are now represented across the road and around the world.

I participate in an Internet chat room and communicate with other Nottingham descendants across the nation. Some of you are here today, and I've spoken with some of you already.

Finally, I believe that the early Nottingham families and their descendants have enriched and blessed this country many times over through their many contributions to our nation and its people. I'm honored today to call you "friend" and to be part of your program to share with you this legacy that began over 300 years ago.

Thank you.

BIBLIOGRAPHY

Beard, Alice. *Births, Deaths and Marriages of the Nottingham Quakers, 1680-1889.* Westminster, MD: Family Line Publications, 1989.

Bradley, A. Day. "Early Settlers of the Nottingham Lots," National *Genealogical Society Quarterly,* Vol. 70 (1982): 282-294.

Fischer, David Hackett. *Albion's Seed: Four British Folkways in America.* New York: Oxford University Press, 1989.

Fisher, Sydney George. *The True William Penn.* Philadelphia: J. B. Lippincott Company, 1900.

Furthey, J. Smith, and Gilbert Cope. *History of Chester County, Pennsylvania: with genealogical and biographical sketches.* Philadelphia: L.H. Everts, 1881.

Johnston, George. *History of Cecil County, Maryland.* Reprint, Baltimore: Genealogical Publishing Company, 1989.

Levy, Barry. *Quakers and the American Family—British Settlements in the Delaware Valley.* Oxford: Oxford University Press, 1988.

Tully, Alan. *William Penn's Legacy—Politics and Social Structure in Provincial Pennsylvania, 1726-1755.* Baltimore: The Johns Hopkins University Press, 1977.

Weeks, Stephen B. *Southern Quakers and Slavery.* Baltimore: The Johns Hopkins Press, 1896.

At the Head of the Bay—A Cultural and Architectural History of Cecil County, Maryland. Baltimore: Cecil Historical Trust, Inc. and Maryland Historical Trust Press, 1996.

Quaker Biographies: A Series of Sketches Chiefly Biographical, Concerning Members of the Society of Friends, from the Seventeenth Century to More Recent Times. Vol. 3. Philadelphia: Friends Book Store, 1909.

Communication with Herbert L. Standing of Earlham, Iowa, former Clerk of Wilmington (Del.) Monthly Meeting, 1964-69 and Quaker historian and genealogist, March, 2001

QUAKER-ROOTS@ rootsweb.com.

John Churchman as told from his Journal

John was a contemporary of and knew John Cadwalader, a mason and builder, from Horsham, Montgomery County, PA traveled with him. John Cadwallader eventually died on the island of Tortolla, while traveling in the ministry.

Edward Hicks, the painter of many peaceable kingdoms, grew up among Friends in Bucks County, PA. He joined Friends and traveled in the ministry, often with the feeling that his carriage painting business was worldly.

Elias Hicks of Jericho, NY, a farmer who is credited with the split among Friends. He felt that God still speaks to all and following the strict Quaker way was not always correct. Elias traveled widely among Friends around his farming operation.

Susanna Morris, from near Abington, PA, who traveled widely in the ministry after her eleven children were able to be cared for without her assistance. She was ship wrecked three times in her travels.

John Woolman of Mt. Holly, NJ was a tailor and helped Friends of the time settle estates. Finding many of his relatives had slaves in their estates bothered him to the point that he spent the rest of his life trying to help others see the evil of slavery. He kept his business small so that he would have time to devote to his calling. He is the most remembered of those working in this cause, as he traveled and met with all in a humble way.

John Churchman was reverent, cheerful and felt the weight of his ministry. He felt called to promote the peaceable kingdom. John was born August 4, 1705 to John and Hannah Seary Churchman of the Nottingham Lots. John felt called early to follow the straight and narrow. He thought, as did many Friends of the time that music diverted the mind from deeper matters. He was afraid to be alone as a child as he felt he was wicked. He learned to read poorly, but at fifteen years some of the fear left and he was able to read and do mathematics well. He still continued to feel that he was not living up to his calling from above, as he had experienced as a small child. At nineteen, while walking to meeting and lamenting that for the last eight years he had not had the contact he desired with God, he felt he wanted to "be made a sanctified vessel and peace be made."

In 1724 his father died and John took over his father's duties at home, although he continued to search for the higher power to lead him. At the age of twenty while he was quite ill, "it pleased the Lord to remember me." He felt his past transgressions were forgiven. "My heart was made exceedingly tender, I wept much, and an evidence was given me, that the Lord had heard my cry." Toward the morning of the fifth day of his illness, "I felt the incomes and owning of divine love in a greater degree than ever." He recovered while noticing the morning light making all "look new and sweet." After this scarcely a day passed without the "feelings of divine life."

At twenty-five he married on January 27 1729/30 at East Nottingham Margaret Brown, "a virtuous young woman, whom I had loved as a sister for several years."

In 1730 Nottingham Monthly Meeting was set apart from New Garden. John felt it was his duty to continue to attend New Garden and did so for many months.

It was also about this time that he was asked to join Friends on family visits. "To some degree he felt the ownings of the Truth. He found that going to meeting for worship a challenge between sleepiness and a roving mind." He felt, "The Lord alone is all-powerful, and worthy to be waited upon and worshipped in humility and reverent adoration of soul for ever."

The love of truth made him willing to attend neighboring meetings and help them "to wait upon God." By 1733 John was named as an elder at Nottingham, and felt called to travel more widely.

At his point the reader should picture a map of the colonies from West River (near Annapolis, MD, where Yearly Meeting was held) to the north as far as New England, as far south as Fairfax and Hopewell, VA, north through the settled meetings in Pennsylvania. Nottingham Quarter spanned both sides of the Susquehanna and John traveled widely to meetings in all of these directions. Eventually he traveled to the British Isles and into Holland in the ministry, especially to Quarterly and Yearly Meetings. He was growing in the knowledge that the Heavenly Father was leading his ministry. In 1735/6 his brother-in-law, William Brown, John's sister Dinah Brown, and John were recommended as ministers.

In 1748 John felt called to visit the mayor of Philadelphia, accompanied with his good friend Israel Pemberton, to lay before the mayor about the nature of his office as magistrate. He was concerned that the "evil doer, drunkards, profane swearers etc. should be encouraged to do well."

Later he met with the Pennsylvania Assembly. He was strongly against raising funds for any war effort. The French & Indian War was looming. This was the time that Friends controlled the Pennsylvania Government. Nottingham was considered to be a part of Pennsylvania. When those in sympathy with the war overruled this body, most Friends resigned rather than be a part of any war.

This particular visit concerned the King of England's insistence of building a place to station a ship of war at the Delaware Capes. John Churchman felt called to go and remind the members of "the danger of departing from trusting in that divine power which had hitherto protected the inhabitants of our land in peace and safety." He had considered this weighty concern for more than a week, before seeking a Friend to help him with the clearness that he should pursue this concern. After the House Speaker had agreed that he could speak, he went in, and after about a twelve minutes of silence he felt led to speak of his concern. He reminded them that the power of God should lead them. The fear of man should not rule.

"May it with gratitude be ever remembered, how remarkably we have been preserved in peace and tranquility for more than fifty years! No invasion by foreign enemies and the treaties of peace with the natives, wisely begun by our proprietor, William Penn, preserved inviolate to this day." He reminded them that the body of government represented many religious groups, but to remember that the charter came first. All should put a humble trust in the divine power. "It is not from disrespect to the king or government that I speak after this manner, for I am thankful I hear that the Lord in mercy hath vouchsafed that the throne of Great Britain should be filled by our present benevolent prince, King George II."

After his speech several members followed him out to express their satisfaction and affection towards his visit. It was during this time that William Brown and John Churchman felt led to travel to Great Britain. They presented their concern to Quarterly Meeting.

He asked the "Lord to enable me, and I will follow thee; it is only by thy strength I can do it." His traveling certificate was signed and in April he traveled to Concord to Quarterly Meeting then on to Philadelphia to seek passage. In June of 1750 he left before sunrise, leaving his dear wife and aged mother behind, and went to Philadelphia that night. While waiting for his passage he visited meetings in the city including the Bank and Market Street Meetings.

On June 6, 1750 they left on the ship Carolina from Chester. William Brown was bothered with seasickness, but John was not. Five weeks later they landed at Dover, England having continued in the Lord's presence with many meetings for worship. As they traveled in the ministry they found some live meetings and some where Friends were "not careful live near the Truth."

These meetings were dull. For four years they traveled around to the meetings in Wales, England, Holland, Scotland, and Ireland. At one of these meetings he felt called to ask a speaker to sit down. Another time he "wanted the true clothing of the Lord's children, which is humility of heart and reverence of spirit."

While traveling with John Pemberton, after visiting meetings with William Brown, where ranterism still prevailed. He also found some Friends living in grandeur and superfluity. John felt led to visit Ireland. After continuing his travels for a week in Ireland, while feeling ill, he decided to send for an apothecary. His illness became "violent." After the bleeding the fever was "somewhat allayed." He fell "into a deep sleep, when I began to bleed again, which brought me very weak, that I was awakened at midnight with great drops of sweat on my face, and sickness. Calling my companion, who watched with me, we found that I had bled much, the orifice in my arm being very large and not carefully bound up. My kind landlord and his wife, being anxious about me, had prevailed with the apothecary to lodge in the house. I desired him to apply a thin piece of bladder as broad as a half-penny on the wound. I asked him to hold his finger on the orifice so as to stop the bleeding, until the plaster dried and stuck . . . He said he had never seen the like. The next morning the physician examined him and after feeling his pulse, decided John was in deep consumption. "He judged my cough to be consumptive and visited daily for a week." The physician advised him to go home as soon as he was able, as he hardly believed John would recover. He told John that he had acted as a mad man, to travel for so long with his fever. "I asked him if he was master of a vessel at sea which had sprung a leak that could not be stopped, what he would do?"

He replied, "endeavor to make the next dry-dock, to unlade the leak."

"Why doctor," said I, "this is my case; I saw no place to lay by until I came hither; at which he laughed, and wished me well."

Upon his return to the colonies, his traveling continued to meetings in Maryland, New Jersey and to Philadelphia Yearly Meeting, but he spent most of the winter at home. He again felt called to protest gathering taxes for the war effort against the Indians. In his letter he reminded Friends that the Prophet foretold the time would come that the "Swords will be beaten into plough-shares, and spears into pruning-hooks." The spirit of the gospel will prevail, which teaches to love enemies and the art of war shall not be learned.

In 1756 the Indians had been burning homes on the frontier. Scalping was a practice and bodies were brought into Philadelphia. John questioned how this could be in the land of peace? In a moment he thought of the enslaved. How could one purchase, sell or keep oppressed people?

He was appointed to visit all of the Quarterly Meetings. The Meetings for Sufferings was established that year. In 1757 he attended the general meeting for ministers and elders in Philadelphia. John continued to travel and meet with Friends throughout the colonies, especially in the Philadelphia Yearly Meeting area.

John's wife, Margaret, had "a cancer of her head" for many years, from which she died. Her memorial written of her death, signed by clerks Samuel England and Rebecca Trimble, stated: she was born of believing parents, they moved to the Nottingham Lots before she was ten. She was religiously inclined from childhood and at thirty-four years of age it pleased the Lord to put her forth in the ministry. She visited families, local meetings, southern provinces and she "exercised to the comfort and edification of the churches where she visited." She was "an example in plainness . . . serviceable in meetings of business . . . with a becoming zeal to support the testimony of Truth in its various branches."

About 1761 he felt he was in his final "sickness." In reviewing his life, he felt that he had "clearly seen that the testimony of Truth, if deeply attended to, will not be found to untie with warlike measures. It will in the Lord's time be exalted above all opposition, and come to possess even the gates of its enemies." Later he added, "divine strength to my soul, that the God of Truth is determined in due time to exalt the mountain of his holiness above all." On Second-day morning 9-11 month he stated; "I have been led to see the necessity there is for Friends to beware of the custom of drinking drams, or strong spirits mixed. It is my judgment, that the less any of us accustom ourselves to the use of those spirits, the better it would be for our constitutions in general. I believe it is not consistent with the will of Divine Providence that the course of nature should be obstructed through the unnatural warmth of spirituous liquors." He recovered from this illness to travel more in the ministry, feeling that he still had a message to deliver. He was concerned that the members were forgetting the ways of Friends. Some of these times he attended meetings when he was not feeling well, but he felt led to continue in his ministry.

His last visit was to the Eastern Shore Meetings and Yearly meeting at Third-Haven in Easton, MD. This meeting was in existence when George Fox, the founder of the Society of Friends of Truth, visited the colonies, as this was one of his stops. "A young man, William Jackson of New Garden Meeting," accompanied John. William's account of this journey in May includes the visit to George Ford's, near Back Creek. The next day's ride was on a damp and foggy morning forty-five miles to Hannah Turner's in Queen Anne's County, where they visited Tuckahoe Meeting. William mentions that John is weak in body, but strong in spirit. They continued their visits into June and finished at London Grove in Chester County, PA before returning to Nottingham. John was glad to return home.

On the 21st of July a Friend came to visit and John remarked: "I feel that which lives beyond death and the grave, which is now an inexpressible comfort to me after a time of deep baptism that I have passed through; I believe my being continued here in the will of Providence, and I am fully resigned." On First-day morning he gave directions about his coffin. On the 24th he had difficulty breathing and expired, having been a minister about forty-two years.

Some of the Churchman family stayed in the Nottingham area. Some were read out of meeting for becoming too interested in scientific things. The above John set a standard for having Nottingham Friends interested in the well being of the members at the expense of the life of the meeting.

John Churchman III knew Thomas Jefferson. There was a dumb waiter in the Churchman stone house that is still standing, just off of 272/273 near the Brick Meeting House in Cecil County, MD.

Paul Rodebaugh gave the talk on the Churchman Journal at the 2001 Tercentenary, but didn't finish the written part of his talk for this book before he died in October 2002 at 61.

Paul was a graduate of West Chester State Teachers College in 1962, having developed an early interest in history. At nineteen he gave his first tour of West Chester and continued with that tradition for 42 years. He was the founder of the West Chester Christmas walk and often led tours through cemeteries, recounting stories of those interred including Civil War soldiers and slaves.

His degree in Geography and American History led to a teaching career for thirty years, at Avon Grove Middle School. He took many of his students west on camping trips and tours to areas such as Yellow Stone National Park and the Grand Canyon. So many shared life stories that he might have called his service a pop corn meeting at his memorial service in West Chester Friends Meeting House on November 10, 2002.

Paul joined the Religious Society of Friends as a young man and soon was involved on several committees. He clerked Quarterly Meeting the Sunday before he died. Historical Friends groups were his favorite interest. At his death he was treasurer of the Parkersville Friends Meeting and on the boards of the Friends Historical Society and the Bible Association of Friends in America. Paul was proud to be able to point out that the Miller family, early Friends at New Garden, tied into his family. He knew where many meeting houses are or were. Many groups invited Paul to speak on various historical issues. Quite often he could tell where the person he spoke of went when they left Chester County and what took them to their new home.

Paul was also a member of the West Chester Rotary Club, the West Chester Bird Club and actively involved as a member of Middletown Preparative Meeting.

Books were his major love. He had over 30,000 volumes and was still happily collecting. In fact he was found with an armload of books where he had fallen when he died.

A Play about William Penn

Performed by George Fox Friends School
2001-2002
Written by Linda Uberseder, Head of school

Cast of Characters

Zack:	Dan Fulmer 10 years old
James Brown:	Sean Stem 5 years old
Sam:	Barb Paparelli 13 years old
Mrs. James Brown:	Lydia Lyon 5 years old
William Penn:	Jakob Moorech 11 years old
Mrs. John Churchman:	B.G. Bond 8 years old
John Churchman:	Avery Sharpless 6 years old
William Brown:	Carmine Zheng 7 years old, John Sylvester 5 years old
Henry Reynolds:	Daniel Merritt 7 years old
Andrew Job:	Suzie McGlinchy 8 years old
Mrs. Reynolds:	Arianna Denison 6 year old
Elizabeth Job:	Heather 5 years old

Zack:	Hey Sam!
Sam:	Hey Zach!
Sam:	Sure is hot today. Let's just hang out under this big tree.
Zach:	Look at this tree! It's huge! It must be really old.
Sam:	Yeah, my mom says its ring dated to 1661. That's over 300 years old! What are you doing?
Zach:	I don't see any old rings hanging on this tree.
Sam:	Not that kind of ring—ring dated means looking at a slice of the tree and counting the rings in it.
Zach:	Oh! 300 years—that's old. I bet only Indians lived around here then.

Sam: Yeah! Mom says it's called a Penn Oak because William Penn brought a bunch of settlers here in 1701 and gave them the land, and the tree was here then.

William Penn Song

(To the tune of *Jesse James*)

William Penn was a man
A Quaker, a Friend
And he owned lots of land, far and wide.
He gave much to his friends
Who came here to settle down
And land for meeting houses set aside.

Zach: William Penn—I thought he founded Pennsylvania?

Sam: He did but this used to be part of it. He divided it up into 37 pieces about 500 acres each.

Zach: Wow that's a lot of land. I think our family has about 1 acre with our house.

Sam: Yeah! I guess everybody was a farmer.

Zach: I wonder what it was like back then?

Sam: Yeah, I wonder?

Little Bird Song

(To the tune of *Kookaberra*)

Little Bird sits in the Penn Oak tree.
Doesn't even know its history.
Watch Little Bird,
Watch Little Bird,
History you will see.

William Penn: We have traveled far friends but we have finally arrived. How does thee like thy new home John Churchman?

John Churchman: It is a wild new place and quite beautiful.

William Penn: I expect you will do well here. I have heard much of your bravery.

John Churchman: Bravery?

William Penn: I speak of the time you chased a herd of wild horses through a dangerous grove of dead trees to retrieve a horse that had been enticed away by them and you a lad of 10 years.

Mrs. Churchman:	Not brave but foolish. I expect I will like it here—a good place to call home when we are not traveling.
William Penn:	What of thee James and William Brown?
James Brown:	This looks like a good place to start an iron works or mill. I think we will be busy.
William Penn:	I heard this family has the skill of masonry. Many homes will be built here.
Mrs. James Brown:	I expect you are right.
Mrs. Reynolds:	How will we decide who gets what land?
William Penn:	We shall draw lots. The one you pick shall be yours. You first Henry Reynolds.
Henry Reynolds:	Oh! The land I have chosen is beautiful. I can stand on it and see my land in all directions! It will be difficult for me to attend meeting here though because of the distance. I will call my home "Graystone" and when I die I will give my son Francis 290 acres in Chichester. John will get 210 acres. Henry will get 410 acres in Nottingham and the girls—Margaret, Prudence, Deborah and Hannah—1 shilling each.
Sam:	Oh Mr. Reynolds?
Henry Reynods:	Yes, my girl?
Sam:	You will go on to found the village of Summer Hill which becomes Rising Sun.
Henry Reynolds:	Will I? How interesting.
William Penn:	What will you do with your land Andrew Job?
Andrew Job:	I think it is a good place to build a tavern. What do you think of the name "The Blue Ball Tavern"? (makes shape)
Zach:	It looks more like a bullet to me!
Elizabehth Job:	A bullet? Good name! We can sit by the fire at night and tell tales of my crazy uncle, Daniel Defoe.
Zach:	Daniel Defoe? Didn't he write *Robinson Crusoe*?
Elizabeth Job:	That he did but he was crazy as a loon. Locked himself up in my mother's house and wouldn't come out.
Henry Reynolds:	I heard he got put in the pillory for writing scandalous pamphlets! I heard you are the sheriff. That kind of thing won't happen here will it?
Andrew Job:	Certainly not!
William Penn:	I think I will set aside this 40 acres here for Friends. I hope someday a meeting house will be built here.
Sam:	Oh it will! It will be called the Brick Meeting House.

William Penn: Very good! Very good!
William Brown: "In humble trust, we begin our labor!"
Zach: Say, a lot of great history happened here.
Sam: Yeah! Look how it's changed since then. Let's go to your house. I'm thirsty.

This Land Is Your Land

(To the tune of *This Land is Your Land*)

This land is your land. This land is my land.
From the Susquehanna
To Rising Sun,
From the Penn's Woods forests
To the deep green valleys,
This land was given by William Penn.

Enjoying a ride in an oxen cart, September 29, 2001. *Photo by Ron Stroud.*

Thoughts on Modern Quaker Faith and Practice

Early Friends experienced a deep and transforming experience of the power of God in their lives. These Friends lived in a time of social upheaval and political chaos. England was entangled in a civil war. The first publication of the Bible in English was made in ____. Many other religious sects and groups were forming and growing.

Today's Friends experience a different world—one of disparities between rich and poor, and a world of many new technologies. Friends struggle to make sense of the tragedies of September 11, 2001.

Quakerism has answers for these issues and for the harder and deeper questions of life. We need to look at our spiritual roots to help people find God and an anchor for their lives.

These are the basic assumptions and convictions of Quakers:

God is real.
God is present everywhere.
God is loving, just and merciful.
God wants to be in relationship with us.
God is immediately available to us.
A relationship with God is not just for our benefit and enjoyment, but also to inspire and enable us to be co-creators of a better world of peace, justice and beauty.
We will not convince others of our Truth by saying it, but by living it. People will look at our lives and ask, "Why are you not afraid? Not lost? Why do you have a sense of direction?"

But, we must also be ready to talk about our religious convictions.

How can we practice our Quaker faith?

1. Make space and time that is open for God—daily. Sunday is not enough for a strong ministry.
2. Connect with resources: scripture, devotional reading, spiritually wise people.

3. Connect with a faith community
4. Listen for Divine Guidance—every day, every moment. Connect with the power, love and guidance of God.
5. Act after listening. Act in love on whatever guidance we have been given.

In short, live day to day with attention to the guidance of God. We Quakers can offer others a Way to find the answers.

Thom Jeavons, General Secretary of Philadelphia Yearly Meeting, spoke on September 30, 2001 from notes. He declined to prepare a text for this publication. These thoughts are based on the notes of a Friend attending Jeavons' presentation.

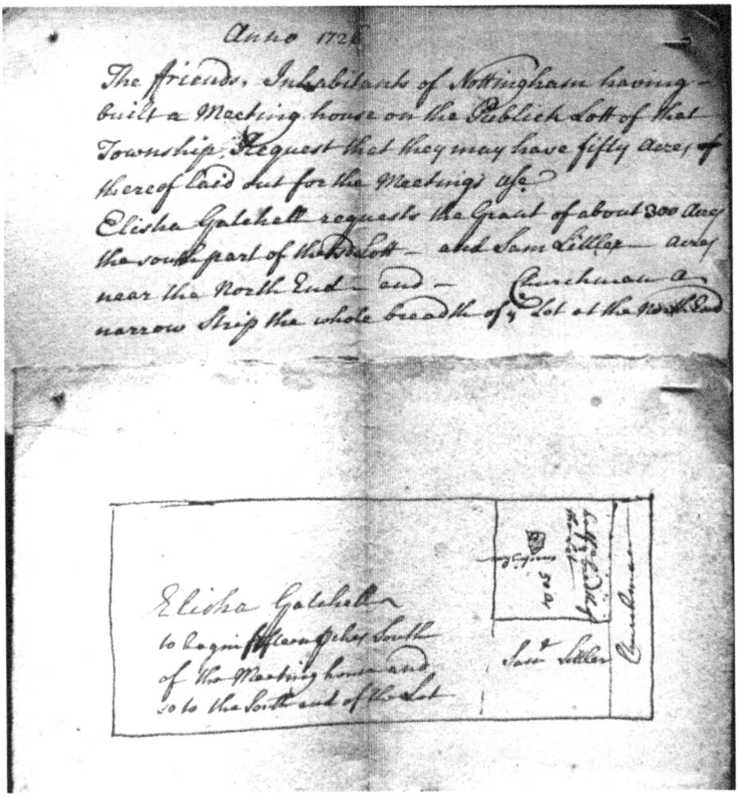
Anno 1726
The friends, Inhabitants of Nottingham having built a Meeting house on the Publick Lott of that Township, Request that they may have fifty acres thereof laid out for the Meetings use.
Elisha Gatchell requests the Grant of about 300 Acres the south part of the sd Lott — and Sam Littler — acres near the North End — and — Churchman a narrow Strip the whole breadth of ye Lot at the North End

The Friends, Inhabitants of the Nottingham having built a Meeting house on the Publick Lot of that Township request that they may have fifty acres thereof laid out for the Meetings use. 1726

FIRST PURCHASERS and SETTLERS of the NOTTINGHAM LOTS

LOTS 1, 7, 9, 13, 21 & 25
PROPRIETARY LANDS

When the "Nottingham Lots" were established, it was requested that 3,000 acres be set aside for the use of the Proprietary Government of William Penn. In addition Lot 30 was established as a common lot for the use of the Nottingham Quakers. In the Pennsylvania Land Records there is a request of the Friends, inhabitants of Nottingham, after having built their meeting house on the public lot, were asking for 50 acres to be laid out for the meeting's use.

LOTS 2 & 3
JOHN GUEST

The Honorable **John Guest**, Esquire, a Quaker from Philadelphia, was one of the purchasers of 1,000 acres of the "Nottingham Lots" in March 1701/02. He was the son of **George** and **Alice Guest**, immigrants from Birmingham, England in 1681. John married **Susannah Welch**, the daughter of **Sarah Welch**, who died before the 1st mo (March) 1705/06., Esq. wrote his will 1 2nd mo (April) 1706 which was probated 22 5th mo (July) 1708 in Philadelphia, PA. It was also recorded in New Castle Co., DE. In his will, John mentions his brothers **Thomas** and **Samuel Guest** and his wife, Susannah. (Philadelphia County Will Book C:113)

LOTS 4 & 18
EDWARD BEESON

Edward Beeson, the son of **Thomas** and **Ann Beeson**, was baptized 24 February 1660 in the parish of Thrussington, Leicestershire, England, where he also married his first wife, **Rachel Pennington** on 24 February 1682. After the death of Rachel, Edward took to wife, **Elizabeth** ________ about 1709. Elizabeth Beeson was with child at the time of her husband's death, which occurred between 20 August 1712, when his will was written and 9 March 1713/14, the date his will was probated. In his Will, he gives to son Edward,

...res of land "laying by Nessamony;" to son Richard, a tract of land near Southampton, Bucks County containing 290 acres, also 25 acres of liberty land by the Schuylkill; to his son William, the west "look" in Nottingham, also, 48 for building him a house and his wearing apparel; and to daughter, Ann Cloud, £20. After his former wife's children have had their portions, the personal estate to be divided between widow (not named) and daughter Elizabeth. His widow was to have the plantation during her widowhood, afterward to daughter Elizabeth. Also provides for the child that wife is "now great with." In his will, Edward Beeson, mentions the land that he purchased of Daniel Wharley. (Chester County, PA Will Book A:1)

Edward Beeson was granted 1,000 acres of the "Nottingham Lots" in March 1701/02 but didn't actually take possession until 1706, when he was granted liberty to settle there. Upon his arrival to the colonies, he settled on the northeast side of the present city of Wilmington not far from the Delaware River. When granted liberty to settle his land in Nottingham Township, Edward Beeson left his home in Delaware to his son, **Edward Beeson, Jr.** and took up his lands in the "Nottingham Lots." It is here, it is thought, that his first wife Rachel died and he married a second time to Elizabeth, although no record has been found to confirm this.

Children of Edward Beeson and Rachel Pennington:

i. Edward, of New Castle Co., DE; md Esther Hall
ii. William, despite his inheritance returned to England
iii. Ann, md John Cloud and lived in Chichester, Chester Co., PA
iv. Richard, md Charity Grubb, daughter of John and Frances Grubb of Marcus Hook, Chester Co., PA, 24 8th mo (December) 1706 at Nottingham Mtg.
Richard and Charity moved to Leacock Twp., Lancaster Co., PA and joined fellowship with the Leacock Meeting.

Children of Richard Beeson and Charity Grubb:

a. John, md 7 8th mo (December) 1733 at Leacock Mtg. Mary Varman, of Leacock Twp.
b. Charity, md Mordecai Mendenhall, son of John Mendenhall of Earl Twp., Lancaster Co., PA, 21 3rd mo (May) 1735 at Leacock Mtg.

Children of Edward Beeson and Elizabeth ________:

v. Elizabeth, md (1) John Everitt ; md (2) Joseph Rich
vi. Rachel, born after 20 6th mo (August) 1712

LOTS 5 &19
HENRY REYNOLDS

Henry Reynolds, the son of **William and Margaret Exton Reynolds**, was born 23 September 1655 in St. Pancras Parish Chichester, Sussex, England, and died 7 6th mo (August) 1724 in Chichester Twp., Chester Co., PA. He was married 10 11th mo (January) 1677/78 to **Prudence Clayton,** at Burlington Monthly Meeting in Burlington Co., NJ. Prudence, the daughter of **William and Prudence Lanckford Clayton**, was born 20 October 1657 in Rumbaldswick, Sussex, England and died before 15 2nd mo (April) 1728 in Chichester Twp., Chester Co., PA.

A patent was granted to Henry Reynolds for 125 acres of land joining his other land on Naaman's Creek. And on 12 November 1683, Henry Reynolds had another 200 acres of land patented to him, extending from the middle branch of Naaman's Creek to the Circular line. He was a publican by trade and kept a tavern in Marcus Hook. He sold liquor there whether he had the courts approval or not. He was a man with a quick temper that often got him in trouble and spent many hours in court. One such case involved the death of his serving girl. At court held in Chester 7 2nd mo (April) 1685, Henry Reynolds took **Justa Anderson** to court for slander. Justa Anderson had stated that Henry had beaten his servant girl and she died the next day of her abuse. The plaintiff showed by **James Sandelands, James Brown** and **William Hawkes** that Justa Anderson stated that he saw Henry Reynolds "beat and kick his maid and that he saw her alive no more." The defendant was able to prove by **Thomas Pearson** that when he was at Reynold's house he saw the latter lift "up the tongs" and threaten to strike the maid servant for not eating such things that were provided for her. **Wooly Rosen**, of Naaman's Creek, New Castle County testified that while he was at Reynolds, the girl asked for some milk, which angered her master, she being an indentured servant, and he struck her with a broom staff, asking her whether there was not victuals enough in the house. Another witness for the plaintiff, **William Cornell**, declared that he saw Reynolds beat his maid with a broom staff and afterwards kicked her as she was by ye fire. **Robert Moulder** related a story that the night the girl died "he see the maid sleeping by ye fireside and sometimes afterwards she went to bed, after which a revelation came to him that the maid would die that night." **Prudence Clayton**, Henry Reynold's mother in law, who after the girl died was called for to lay the body out, did not remember that she saw any hurt about her. The jury found for the defendant, which raised such public attention that **James Kenneily**, the first coroner of Chester County, intervened in the matter. At court held 3 7th mo (September) 1685, "Execution be granted against Henry Reynolds for ye Crowner's fee, charges of the inquest, with all other charges whatsoever thereunto belonging."

By deed dated 10 December 1700, Henry Reynolds granted to **Roger Jackson** 43 acres in Chichester, which was part of a 47-acre tract that Henry had purchased of William Clayton. The tract was bounded by Chester Creek and the property of Joseph Pyle.

Along with other adventurous Quakers, Henry Reynolds was granted 1000 acres of land in the "Nottingham Lots" in March 1701/02. He requested of the Proprietary a small vacancy joining the west side of his "Lot" by the side of a Creek, containing about 50 acres, on which he and **Messer Brown** planned to build a grist mill for the convenience of that end of the township. He also requested a grant of a vacancy on the north side of Nottingham Township of about 100 acres.

Henry Reynolds, of Chichester, wrote his will 12 2nd mo (April) 1720 and it was probated 16 October 1724. It is not known whether he and Prudence ever moved to the Nottingham Lots or stayed in Chichester, where they died. In his will he leaves his son Francis the plantation on where "I live in Chichester", containing 290 acres, he paying his brother William when 21, £20; to his son John, a tract of land in Chichester, containing 210 acres, he paying his brother, William, £20; to son Henry, tract of land in Nottingham containing 490 acres, and to son William, tract of land in Nottingham, it being the south "Lot", containing 490 acres. To each of his daughters, Margaret, Prudence, Deborah and Hannah, 1 shilling each. And to wife, Prudence, all personal estate. (Chester Co., PA Will Book A:164)

Prudence Reynolds wrote her will 17 9th mo (November) 1726 and had it probated 15 April 1728. In it, she leaves to her daughter, "as many as shall be in being" all household goods. To son Francis' eldest son, Henry, one silver cup valued at 40 shillings. Remainder of estate to all children in being, none named. (Chester Co., PA Will Book A:274)

Children of Henry Reynolds and Prudence Clayton:

i. Margaret, born 25 5th mo (July 1680) in Chester Co., PA; md ______ Moulder.
It is thought that his name was Benjamin Moulder, but there has been no proof presented to date to confirm that assumption.

ii. Mary, born 13 9th mo (November) 1682 in Chester Co., PA; md Isaac Sharp

iii. Francis, born 15 8th mo (October) 1684 in Chester Co., PA; md to Elizabeth Acton 29 10th mo (December) 1712 in Salem Mtg., Salem Co., NJ; died in January 1760 in Chester Co., PA

Children of Francis Reynolds and Elizabeth Acton:

a. Prudence, born 16 1st mo (March) 1713/14; md John Dutton 4 October 1733 at Chichester Mtg.

b. Lydia, born 24 2nd mo (April) 1716 in Chester Co., PA; md (1) Joseph Talbot; md (2) Joseph Townsend 17 3rd mo (May 1739) in Chichester Mtg.
c. Christian, born 22 4th mo (June) 1718; md John Hoopes 20 8th mo (October) 1743 in Chichester Mtg.
d. Henry, born 12 4th mo (June) 1720; md Sarah Davis, dau John and Rebekah Davis, 2 7th mo (September) 1751 in Darby Mtg.; died 17 November 1756 in Chichester Twp., Chester Co., PA and is buried in Friends burial ground at Chichester
e. Benjamin, born 26 8th mo (October) 1722; md (1) Sarah Baker; and md (2) Phebe White 26 August 1792 [she died 10 August 1803]; died 26 September 1798
f. John, born 12 10th mo (December) 1725
g. Samuel, md Jane Jones
h. On 4 March 1772 he and his family was granted a certificate to Wilmington Friends Mtg. from Chichester Mtg.
h. Francis

iv. Prudence, born 20 3th mo (May) 1687 in Chester Co., PA
v. Deborah, born 16 4th mo (June) 1689 in Chester Co., PA
vi. William, born 30 5th mo (July) 1691 in Chester Co., PA; died before 5 7th mo (September) 1701 in Chester Co., PA
vii. Henry, Jr., born 16 6th mo (August) 1693 in Chichester Twp., Chester Co., PA; md (1) Hannah Brown, who died in West Nottingham Twp., Cecil Co., PA 1717; (2) Ann Worley; (3) Mary Coles, widow of Jacob Haines; died 17 10th mo (December) 1779 in West Nottingham Twp., Cecil Co., MD. Mary Coles was born 4 3rd mo (May) 1708, the daughter of William and Mary Royal Coles. It should be noted here that Mary Royal was one of the "stolen children of Scotland" and was kidnapped in 1697. After transportation to Pennsylvania, her indenture was sold to **Caleb Pusey**. Mary Royal md (1) **William Coles**, who died in 1710 in Nottingham Twp., Chester Co., PA; and md (2) **Jeremiah Brown**.

Henry Reynolds received a Penn Grant for ten farms on every side of his father's estate. There were 300 acres deeded to him on 7 October 1737 and another 145 acres were deeded to Henry Reynolds in 1741. He is reputed to be the founder of the borough of Rising Sun, originally called Summer Hill. Henry found it increasingly difficult to attend meeting at the Brick Meetinghouse at Calvert, due to "the great distance" he had to travel, so he founded the West Nottingham Meeting on the west side of Rising Sun, nearer to his home. Henry Reynolds was a minister among Friends.

Children of Henry Reynolds and his first wife, Hannah Brown:

a. Rachel, born 6 11th mo (January) 1717/18 in Chester Co., PA; md (1) John Piggott 21 10th mo (December) 1737; md (2) to Thomas Churchman, son of John (dec'd) and Hannah (Seary) Churchman 5 4th mo (June)1745 at Nottingham Mtg.; died 31 11th mo (January) 1756
b. William, born 22 1st mo (March) 1721 in Chester Co., PA; md Prudence Haines, dau of Jacob and Mary (Coles) Haines 5 3rd mo (May) 1743 at Nottingham Mtg.
c. Samuel, 26 8th mo (October) 1723 in Chester Co., PA; md to Susanna Sidwell, dau of Richard Sidwell 25 1st mo (March) 1747 at Nottingham Mtg.
Samuel Reynolds had settled in Little Britain Twp., Lancaster Co., PA before his marriage.
d. Henry, born 1 2nd mo (April) 1725 in Chester Co., PA; md to Mary Haines, daughter of Jacob (dec'd) and Mary (Coles) Haines 29 2nd mo (April) 1747 at Nottingham Mtg.; died in April 1809 W. Nottingham Hundred, Cecil Co., MD
e. Jacob Reynolds, born 14 7th mo (September) 1728 in Chester Co.; md Rebekah Daye, daughter of John and Lydis (Ross) Daye 10 August 1751 at Nottingham Mtg; died 6 February 1799 in W. Nottingham Twp., Cecil Co., MD
f. Joseph, born 31 6th mo (August) 1730 in Chester Co., PA; md Sarah Haines dau Jacob and Mary (Coles) Haines 27 February 1755 at Nottingham Mtg.; died 19 July 1760 in Philadelphia, PA

Children of Henry Reynolds and his third wife, Mary Coles:

g. Benjamin, born 30 11th mo (January) 1743/44 in West Nottingham Twp., Chester Co., PA; md Mary Job
h. Isaac, born 20 5th mo (July) 1745 in West Nottingham Twp., Chester Co., PA; md Ann Rich
i. John, born 20 5th mo (July) 1745, twin to Isaac, in West Nottingham Twp., Chester Co., PA; md Rachel Cowgale 10 September 1778
j. Jesse, born 22 8th mo (October) 1747 in West Nottingham Twp., Chester Co., PA; md to Sarah Haines, daughter of William and Lydia (Johnson) Haines 31 January 1770 at St. James Episcopal Church, Lancaster, PA; died 2 June 1804 in West Nottingham Twp., Cecil Co., MD
Sarah Haines was born 8 4th mo (June) 1751 in W. Nottingham Twp., Chester Co., PA

k. David, born 27 3rd mo (May) 1750 in West Nottingham Twp., Chester Co., PA; md Catherine ______
l. Elijah Reynolds, born 2 February 1753 in West Nottingham Twp., Chester Co., PA

viii. John, born 21 12th mo (February 1694/95) in Chester Co., PA; md Martha ______ in June 1727; died circa 1730 in Chichester Twp., Chester Co., PA. He married out of unity with Friends. It appears that he was disciplined for his marriage by a priest, and remained a Quaker for the Chichester meeting record gives us a glimpse into the life of Martha Reynolds. "Martha Reynolds, for many years a widow, having taken into her house as a servant a person that was a stranger to most of the Meeting and since delivered of a child by him." She was disowned 2 August 1736.

ix. Hannah, born 11 11th mo (January) 1696/97 in Chester Co., PA; md Richard Brown 30 8th mo (October) 1717 at Chichester Mtg.; died 13 3rd mo (May) 1726 in Chester Co., PA

x. William, born 5 7th mo (September) 1701 in Chester Co., PA; md (1) Mary Brown 23 11th mo (January) 1723/24 and: md (2) Rachel Johns 19 10th mo (December) 1739

Children of William Reynolds and Mary Brown:

a. Jeremiah, born 23 11th mo (January) 1725/26
b. David, born 1 1st mo (March) 1727/28
c. Catherine, born 1 12th mo (February) 1729/30; died in 1731
d. Hannah, born 1 9th mo (November) 1733; md ______ Cook; died 19 January 1758
e. Jonathan, born 5 7th mo (September) 1735; died 9 march 175_
f. William, born 15 11th mo (January) 1737/39
g. Mary, born 15 11th mo (January) 1737/39 (twin to William); died in 1737

Child of William Reynolds and Rachel Johns:

h. Thomas, born 10 3rd mo (May) 1742

LOTS 6 & 20
JOHN RICHARDSON

John Richardson is listed as one of the purchasers who purchased the "Nottingham Lots" in March 1701/02. He never resided on the Lots that he purchased. In Ashmead's *History of Delaware County, PA*, John is listed as a justice of New Castle Co. [DE]. He, along with **Cornelius Empson** and **Richard Halliwell**, also justices of New Castle Co., and **Caleb Pusey**, **Philip Roman** and **Robert Pyle**, justices for Chester County, met with **Isaac Taylor**, surveyor for Chester County [PA] and **Thomas Pierson**, surveyor for New Castle County [DE] and, "In their presence to admeasure and survey from the town of New Castle the distance of twelve miles in a right line up ye said river from ye said distance according to ye Kings letters patent and deeds from the Duke and ye said circular line to be well marked two thirds parts of ye semicircle." On 24 November 1725, John Richardson requested a grant of swamp land or cripple adjoining the upper part of his land on the north side of Christiana Creek.

In the records for the Center Monthly Meeting, in New Castle Co., DE, we find that John Richardson was an active member of that meeting. The 7 3rd mo (May) 1709 meeting had been held at his house. On 4 3rd mo (May) 1715, he, along with **Joel Baily**, **Howell James**, and **Alphonusus Kirk** were appointed to attend the Quarterly Meeting and, on 2 6th mo (August) 1718, John was, again, appointed to attend the Quarterly Meeting with **Joel Baily**, **Thomas Hollingsworth** and **John Husey**.

LOTS 8 & 24
CORNELIUS EMPSON
AND
LOTS 10 & 22
EBENEZER EMPSON

Cornelius Empson is thought to have been born about 1660 in Goole Parish, West Riding, Yorkshire, England, the son of **Richard** and **Mary (Clark) Empson**. He died in New Castle County, DE in 1710/11. Cornelius Empson was married four times. His first wife, **Mary Sanderson**, lived long enough to bear him three children. She died 30 11th mo (January) 1688/89. At the Monthly meeting held at Newark during December 1689, Cornelius Empson and **Elizabeth Sanderson** signified their intention to marry. Their request was taken into serious consideration and it was determined that they "could in no wise be joyned with by ye meeting by reason of their nearness of kin, she being his former wife's own sister." They married against the wishes of the meeting for which Cornelius was severely disciplined. At the Newark Monthly Meeting held 1 1st mo (March) 1689/70 it was the judgement of the meeting that he "ought not come amongst us any more in our men's meeting until he gives satisfaction for his own doing." The meeting, which had been held at his house, was withdrawn until such time as he gave satisfaction for his misdeed. This must have been a crushing blow to Cornelius, who had been very active in the affairs of the Newark Meeting, so much so, that on 7 June 1670, he sent a paper of his condemnation to the meeting asking that he be allowed fellowship among Friends again. He must have been successful for in March

1691, Cornelius was again involved in the workings of the Monthly Meeting. On 4 12th mo (February) 1691/92, Cornelius Empson again asked the Meeting for a "certificate of clearness to marry," his second wife, Elizabeth, having recently died. His request was granted this time, but it was almost a year before he chose his next wife. And when he did, he presented his certificate to the Chesterfield Meeting in Burlington Co., NJ and there married **Sarah Wilson**, daughter of **Robert Wilson**, in April 1693. They returned to New Castle Co., DE to live where Sarah died about 1702 and Cornelius Empson married a fourth time to **Mary Richardson** at Salem Meeting after 25 8th mo (October) 1703, when Cornelius presented his "certificate" to the meeting.

By today's standards Cornelius Empson would be considered a "big operator." He was always undertaking new projects. He built several mills and speculated in land. Cornelius was very active in the civil affairs of New Castle Co., DE and was commissioned a Justice of the Peace and Judge of the Courts in 1685 and 1701. He also was a member of the Provincial Council in 1686, 1693, 1695, 1696 and 1697 and a judge of the Supreme Court of Pennsylvania from 1689-1701.

Cornelius Empson settled on the east side of the Brandywine in New Castle Co., DE in 1682, along with **Valentine Hollingsworth**, **William Stockdale**, **Thomas Conoway**, **Adam Sharpley**, **Morgan Durett** and **Valentine Morgan**. On 2 June 1685, he bought from **Mary Block**, **Barbara Maislander** and **Christian Stalcap** 78 acres of "fast land" that had been resurveyed 23 October 1680. It was at the head of Shellpot Creek and on both sides and adjoined Vertrechts Hook. This land included a grist mill and in May 1688, Cornelius Empson made an agreement with ______ **Salif** and **Erasmus Stidham** "for free grinding of corn for them and their horses." In 1690 Cornelius Empson was authorized to erect a ferry over the Brandywine Creek.

In November 1701, Cornelius Empson, along with others to the number of 20 families, chiefly of Chester County, presented a petition to the Commissioner of Property at Philadelphia requesting enough land to make a settlement "on a tract of land" about half way between the Delaware and Susquehannah Rivers or nearer the latter, being about 24 miles from New Castle. They were asking for 20,000 acres of land in the said place at a "bushel of wheat per 100 acres rent or, 5 purchase, to be after at a shilling per annum." To encourage the settlement of the lands near the Susquehannah River, it was proposed that they could have 15 to 20,000 acres at £8 per 100 acres or at 2 bushels of wheat per annum rent. The first year to be free of rent or one year credit to pay the purchase money. An agreement was reached and this land became the "Nottingham Lots" and on 1 March 1701/02, a warrant was issued for this land. Eighteen divisions were to be made, each containing 1,000 acres. Cornelius Empson, nor his son, Ebenezer, lived on the "Lots," preferring to live in New Castle County, Delaware.

By his will dated 12 December 1710, Cornelius bequeathed to his son Richard, five shillings, "which shall be in full of all his portion," so that he nor his heirs have any more demand of the estate, real or personal; he bequeathed to his son Ebenezer, ten shillings and the Negro boy Zaharias, "which shall be in full of all his portion," so that he nor his heirs have any more demand of the estate, real or personal; to daughters Sarah and Elizabeth, one Moiety and half of the mill on White Clay Creek for them and their heirs forever; to daughter, Sarah my Mulatto girl Henn; to daughter Elizabeth, my Negro girl Abigail; to son Charles, the easterly part of my plantation containing about 400 acres more or less; to son Charles, half part of a grant called "Chestnut Hill" with the housing and all the cleared land; also to son Charles, one Negro boy called Robbin; to son James, plantation called "Horse Hooke" containing 300 acres more or less lying on the west side of Rook Creek on Brandywine; to son James, on Mulatto boy called Andrew; with James to give his sister, Susannah, £30 silver money when she arrives at the age of 23; he bequeathed to wife Mary and daughters Ann & Susannah, all his personal estate to be shared equally; wife Mary and daughters Ann & Susannah to pay to daughter Mary, £80 silver money when she arrives at the age of 21; his wife Mary shall have full use of the plantations during her widowhood and all the Negroes given to said children who are not of age, until they arrive at the age of 21. If my wife should marry, then she is to deliver all property, real and personal, to the hands of the executors until the children obtain the age of 21. She is also to have £100 and a Negro woman named Grace after her marriage and no more; his daughter Mary, to have a Mulatto girl named Mall; Eight thousand foot of boards at the White Clay creek mill shall be for the use of his wife, if she paid for the cutting and hauling of the timber. Son Charles to be paid £200 should the real estate be sold by the executors. (New Castle Co., DE Wills)

Cornelius Empson was a man of rare courage and persistence. He was a true pioneer, helping in his own way to build a nation and oversee its laws.

Children of Cornelius Empson and his first wife, Mary Sanderson:

i. Richard
ii. Ebenezer, died in 1726; md Susannah Wood, daughter of Joseph Wood, of New Castle Co., DE

Children of Ebenezer Empson and his wife Susannah Wood

a. William, born 1715; md 23 9th mo (November) 1739 at Concord Mtg. to Martha Taylor, spinister, dau of John Taylor; will probated in New Castle Co., DE in 1762
b. Jonathan, born 1719; died 1723
c. Mary, born 1720

d. Rebecca, born 1722
e. Susannah, born 1724

iii. Sarah

Children of Cornelius Empson and his third wife, Sarah Wilson

iv. Elizabeth
v. Mary

Children of Cornelius Empson and his fourth wife, Mary Richardson

vi. Charles
vii. James
viii. Ann
ix. Susannah

LOT 11
JOEL BAILY

Joel Baily was baptized in Bromham Parish, Wiltshire, England, the son of **Daniel** and **Mary** ________ **Baily (Bayly)**. Daniel Baily (Bayly) was a broad weaver in Westbrook, Bromham Parish, and this is where Joel grew up and learnt his trade, as a weaver. The death of Joel Baily occurred in Marlborough Twp., Chester Co., PA between 9 December 1731, when he wrote a codicil to his will and 8 April 1732, when his will was probated. Joel was married to **Ann Short**, the daughter of ________ **Short** and **Miriam Ingram**. Ann Short is generally accepted as being a passenger on the "Welcome" with **William Penn** in the 1682 migration. Her uncle, **Isaac Ingram**, a definite passenger, died on the trip over and left all his worldly goods to his sister, Miriam Short's three children, Adam, Ann and Miriam, his sister, Miriam, lately deceased. **Miriam Short** married shortly after the "Welcome" landed in Upland to **George Thompson**, another Welcome passenger. Ann Short was born after 11 April 1687 in England and died before 10 December 1728, when Joel Baily wrote his will. She is not mentioned in it.

The first that we find of Joel Baily in Pennsylvania is in his representation of a warrant of land belonging to Daniel Baily (Bayly) 25 November 1684. "At the request of Joel Bayley on behalf of Daniel Bayley in right of **William Smith**, of Brumhamhouse, purchaser, what we would grant him [Daniel Baily/Bayly] to take up one hundred twenty five acres of Land in the County of Chester." William Smith had purchased 1,250 acres of land from William Penn and by deeds dated 19 & 20 October 1681 sold 125 acres to Daniel Bayly of Westbrook. The land was located in Birmingham Twp., Chester Co., PA and was subsequently sold to **John Radley**. Joel first settled on 50 acres of land in Middletown Twp. that he purchased from **James Craft** 7 September 1688, which he and his wife, Ann sold to **Thomas Dutton**, of Ashton, by deed dated 8 September 1713. By this time he is listed as living in Marlborough Twp, Chester County. We find that Joel Baily is listed as one of the first purchasers of 500 acres of the "Nottingham Lots" in March 1701/02, although he never lived there. It is hard to say, with accuracy, whether Joel Baily took possession of his lot. He did not bequeath it to any of his heirs in his will. His will was written 10 December 1728 with a codicil written 9 December 1731/32 and probated 8 April 1732. Joel bequeathed to his son Daniel, £8; son Joel was to receive £4; son Thomas to receive 193 acres of land in Marlborough Twp., part of 400 acres brought from Richard Barnard; son John to receive the remainder of 207 acres of said tract; son Josiah to receive "my new dwelling plantation" of 100 acres, he paying his brother Thomas £15; to daughters Mary and Ann, each £10 and to grand daughter, Ann Stewart, £10. In the codicil, Joel Baily directs that son Josiah to pay his sister Mary Harlan £10 and divides the 400 acres equally between John and Thomas. (Chester Co., PA Will Book A:363)

Children of Joel Baily and his wife Ann Short:

i. Mary, born 10 9th mo (November) 1688 in Chester Co., PA; md (1) Alexander Stewart about 1707 died before 20 October 1741 in Bradford Twp., Chester Co., PA. She is buried at Friends graveyard at Bradford. Alexander Stewart was "one of the Stolen Children of Scotland" and was kidnaped in 1697 and transported to Pennsylvania by William Trent. His indenture was sold to Francis Chadsey 5 October 1697 for a term of 8 years if he "be taught to read and write" Francis Chadsey sold the indenture of Alexander to Henry Nayle to teach him the trade of a shoemaker. Alexander Stewart was not a member of the Quakers and when Mary Baily married him, she was disowned for "marrying out of unity" with Friends. When Alexander died in 1714, Mary was rejoined with the Quakers and on 5 November 1715, she condemned her misconduct in marrying out of unity. In February 1715/16, she married (2) George Harlan at Kennett Meeting.

Children of Mary Baily and her husband, Alexander Stewart:

a. Jane; born in 6th mo (August) 1709 in Kennett Twp., Chester Co., PA; md Josiah Taylor 14 3rd mo (May) 1730 in Chester Co., PA
b. Robert, born 25 11th mo (January) 1710/11 in Kennett Twp., Chester Co., PA; 1783 in Georgia; md Martha Richardson in 1732
c. Ann, born 4 6th mo (August) 1712; md Henry Marsh
d. Mary, born 8 3rd mo (May) 1714; md Joseph Taylor

Children of Mary Baily and her husband, George Harlan:

- e. John, born in 1716
- f. Rebecca, born in 1718
- g. Dinah, born in 1720
- h. Hannah
- i. Joel Harlan, born 10 11th mo (January) 1724/25; died 3 September 1796; buried at W. Bradford Friends burying ground
- j. Michael
- k. George, md Susanna Harlan, dau of Ezekiel Harlan, 14 9th mo (November) 175 at London Grove Mtg.

- ii. Anne, born 10 10th mo (December) 1691 in Chester Co., PA; died 12 August 1774 in Chester Co., PA; md in June 1710 in Center Mtg. to Jeremiah Cloud
- iii. Daniel, born 3 10th mo (December) 1693 in Chester Co., PA; md 16 1st mo (March) 1720/21 at Goshen Mtg. to Olive Harris, dau of Hugh Harris, late of Birmingham Twp., Chester Co., PA; died in 1783 in E. Marlborough Twp., Chester Co., PA
- iv. Isaac, born 24 10th mo (December) 1695 in Chester Co., PA; md 1 March 1726/27 Abigail Johnson, dau of Robert Johnson; died bef. 5 8th mo (October) 1732 in Marlborough Twp., Chester Co., PA. Abigail was born 17 October 1700 in Coleboy, Co. Wicklow, Ireland
- v. Joel, born 17 12th mo (February) 1696/97 in Chester Co., PA; md 28 8th mo (October) 1724 Betty Caldwell; died about 1775 in W. Marlborough Twp., Chester Co., PA
- vi. John, born about 1699 in Chester Co., PA; md (1) 29 3rd mo (May) 1729 Lydia Pusey, dau of William Pusey of London Grove, Chester Co., PA (2) 8 June 1732 Mary Marsh
- vii. Thomas, born about 1700 in Chester Co., PA; md Sarah Bentley; died in 1764 in Newlin Twp., Chester Co., PA
- viii. Josiah, born in Chester Co., PA; md 9 3rd mo (May) 1734 at Sadsbury Mtg. to Sarah Marsh; died 14 January 1791 in W. Marlborough Twp., Chester Co., PA

LOTS 12 & 26
JAMES COOPER

James Cooper was born in England and when he arrived in Pennsylvania about 1683; he was listed as being from Mayfield, Staffordshire, England. James and his future wife came over as servants, perhaps to obtain the 50 acres guaranteed to them by William Penn for those who served in that capacity. He married (1) **Hannah** ________ about 1698 and (2) **Mary Ludwedge** 8

November 1705 at St. Paul's Church in Chester. Court records show that Mary Ludwedge had been assigned to him as a servant, by Jasper Yeats, on 28 August 1705. James Cooper died after 1728, most likely in New Castle Co., DE, but there are no records of his death or burial to date. It should be noted that until the death of his first wife, Hannah, James Cooper was a member of the Society of Friends. But, in the 1704-1705 membership rolls of the St. Paul's Church in Chester, he is listed with his second wife, Mary.

We can follow James Cooper through his land transactions. In the minutes of the commissioners of property, 21 January 1701/01, **James** and **Hannah Cooper**, **Robert Scothorn**, **Henry Giles**, **Francis Crompton**, **Daniel Hybert**, **John Marshall**, **Robert Smith**, **Jno. Kirk**, **John Roads**, **Thomas Collier** and **John Ball**, having all come as servants in 1682 & 1683, as by the certificates of **John Blunston**, appeared and requested their head of land according to the Proprietor's engagement. Ordered to the first six one warrant and the last six another for 300 acres, each, to be laid out in the township allotted for servants. There was no actual township laid out for this purpose, but it is thought that James Cooper's land was in Darby Township as he is involved in the affairs of others of that township. In March 1701/02 he was one of the first purchasers of 1000 acres at £8 per annum of the "Nottingham Lots" and was listed as James Cooper, of Darby Twp. No records have been found that he ever lived on this property. In 1719, James Cooper was listed as a "cloth worker" or fuller by trade when he purchased 150 acres in New Castle Co., DE on the White Clay Creek. He called his plantation "Muscle Cripple Plantation."

Children of James Cooper and his wife Hannah ________ :

i. Mary, born 3 9th mo (November) 1699; md James Johnson of New Garden, in 1721.
ii. William, born 11 July 1701; md 18 8th mo (October) 1730 at Sadsbury Mtg. to Mary Miller, dau of Samuel and Margaret Miller of Sadsbury Twp., Chester Co., PA.

Children of James Cooper and Mary Ludwedge:

iii. Calvin, a fuller by trade, born abt 1706; md (1) **Phebe Hall**, daughter of Samuel and Anna Elizabeth Hall of Kennett, 29 4th mo (June) 1732; died 15 September 1779 in Sadsbury Twp. They lived first at Birmingham where Calvin was an overseer of the poor in 1734. A deed for a farm of 150 acres of land in Sadsbury Twp., Chester Co., PA was granted to Calvin Cooper on 28 January 1734/35. He and family moved to this farm and united with Friends at the Sadsbury Meeting. In 1743 he and others were appointed to divide the township of Sadsbury. He was elected as a county commissioner in 1747, and then elected to the Assembly 1749 to 1754. In 1756, he was appointed, with others, to look after the "poor Acadians," who had been driven from their homes and scattered through Pennsylvania and other provinces. He was commissioned a justice of the court of common pleas in 1759. Phebe (Hall) Cooper died 18 June 1757 and Calvin md (2) a widow, **Elizabeth Jeffries**, in 1758.

Children of Calvin Cooper and his wife, Phebe Hall:

a. William, born 5 9th mo (November) 1734; md **Elizabeth Pyle**; died 20 February 1821
b. George, born 28 12th mo (February) 1737; md **Susanna Truman**; died 14 January 1820
c. John, born 9 12th mo (February) 1739; md **Rebecca Moore**; died 25 February 1811
d. Hannah, born 3 10th mo (December) 1742
e. Mary, born 17 12th mo (February) 1744; md (1) **John Dixon** and (2) **James Philips**; died 18 September 1806
f. James, born 14 12th mo (February) 1747; md (1) **Rachel Moore** and (2) **Catherine Powell**
g. Phebe, born 6 6th mo (August) 1750
h. Sarah, born 12 December 1753; md **Thomas Dixon**
i. Hannah md **John Clark** 8 March 1738/39

LOTS 14 & 27
JAMES BROWN

James Brown was born 27 May 1656/57 near Wellingborough, Northamptonshire, England, the son of **Richard** and **Mary ________ Brown** and died in December 1715 in East Nottingham Twp., Chester Co., PA. He was married under a sailcloth 8 6th mo (August) 1679 to **Honor Clayton** at Burlington Mtg., Burlington Co., NJ. Their wedding was reported to be the first wedding held at the Burlington Mtg, which had been held under a sailcloth, most likely from the ship "Kent" before a meeting house was built. Honor was the daughter of **William** and **Prudence (Lanckford) Clayton** and was born 29 November 1662 in Sussex Co., England.

James Brown purchased 1000 acres of mostly woodland and marsh, located in Chichester Twp., Chester Co., PA from **Woole Rawson** on 1 March 1685. Chester County court records from 1697-1710 show that many lots of one to nine acres were sold in Chichester by James Brown, but there is mention of one acre cleared for the use as a burial ground. On 15 September 1699 James and Honor Brown of Chichester, sold 21 acres of woodland and eight acres of marshland for £100 to Peter Boss. Another nine acre woodland lot was given to Chichester on 24 February 1702 for two streets and a road on the south side of town.

In the Spring of 1701, an advance search party of **Henry Reynolds**, **William** and **James Brown**, **John Churchman**, **John Richardson**, **Joel Baily** and **James Cooper** traveled to the area now known as the "Nottingham Lots" to examine the area of the Northeast and Octoraro Creeks. A year later, in March 1701/02, the land was purchased and settlement had begun (see **Cornelius Empson**).

James Brown wrote his will 15 11th mo (January) 1715. In it he bequeathed to his sons William & Jeremiah, daughter Margery Piggott, grandson James, son of William, grandchildren Patience & Jeremiah, children of son Jeremiah, granddaughter Margery, daughter of Margery and John Piggott, each to receive £5, the grandchildren to receive their portion when they reach the age of 21 years; to son Daniel the lot of land between Dorson's and **Robert Williams** containing 500 acres; to daughter Mary Brown £20 when she reached the age of 20 years; to wife Honor and son James, the remainder of estate, paying all legacies. Nothing is to be done without the consent of Mercer (Messer) Brown and son Jeremiah Brown. The will was probated 1 January 1715/16. (Chester Co. Will Book A:30).

Children of James Brown and Honor Clayton:

i. James, born 17 1st mo (March) 1680/81 in Chester Co., PA; died in Bladen Co., NC

ii. William, born 13 1st mo (March) 1681 in Marcus Hook, Chester Co., PA; died before October 1716 in Principio, Cecil Co., MD; md 4 6th mo (August) 1704 Esther (Hester) Baker at Falls Mtg., Bucks Co., PA. Esther Baker was the dau of Henry and Margaret (Hardman) Baker

Children of William Brown and Esther Baker:

a. William, born 1705 in Chester Co., PA; md 11 2nd mo (April) 1728 Susanna Churchman, dau of John and Hannah (Seary) Churchman; died 28 May 1786. Susanna was born 13 7th mo (September) 1701 in Chester Co., PA; died 25 August 1790 in Bel Air, Harford Co., MD

b. Margaret, born 13 1st mo (March) 1706/07 in Chester Co., PA; md 27 11th mo (January) 1728/29 to John Churchman; died 28 July 1770. John Churchman was born 4 August 1705 in Chester Co., PA, the son of John and Hannah (Seary)

Churchman; died 24 July 1775 in E. Nottingham Hund., Cecil Co., MD

c. Daniel, born 1708 in Chester Co., PA; md (1) Susanna Oldham and (2) 3 3rd mo (May) 1753 Susanna Elgar, dau of Joseph and Mary Elgar; died 26 December 1791 in VA. She Susanna Elgar died in August 1805 in Winchester, VA

d. James, born about 1712; md Miriam Churchman, dau of John and Hannah (Seary) Churchman; died 4 March 1772 in Wilmington, DE

e. Ebenezer

f. Esther

iii. Clayton, born 5 8th mo (October) 1685 in Marcus Hook, Chester Co., PA; md 8 8th mo (October) 1748 Mary Robbins at Burlington Mtg, Burlington Co., NJ

iv. Jeremiah, born 1687 in Marcus Hook, Chester Co., PA; md (1) 12 2nd mo (April) 1711 Mary Royal, widow of William Coles and (2) Mary Winter; died 7 March 1767 in Nottingham, Chester Co., PA

Children of Jeremiah Brown and Mary Royal:

a. Patience, born 25 5th mo (July) 1712 in Chester Co., PA; died 23 May 1783 in Cane Creek, NC

b. Jeremiah, born 2 12th mo (February) 1713/14 in Chester Co., PA

c. Joshua, born 5 3rd mo (May) 1717 in Chester Co., PA; md Hannah Gatchell dau Elisha and Sarah (Churchman) Gatchell; died in Little Britain Twp., Lancaster Co., PA. In the "Friends Miscellany" Joshua Brown and his wife, Hannah, visited various Friends meetings in the South. At a place called 'Ninety Six' in South Carolina, they were put in prison on suspicion of being spies. Because of their Quaker principles, they refused to post bond or to take any oath. They were finally released and Joshua Brown returned to his 'habitation 26 day 12th month (December) 1778, with a quiet and thankful mind.'

d. Isaac, born 20 3rd mo (May) 1720; md 3 9th mo (November) 1743 Lydia Slater, daughter of George and Sarah Slater; died 23 January 1781 in Cecil Co., MD

v. Margery, born 1689 in Marcus Hook, Chester Co., PA); md 18 1st mo (March) 1713/14 John Piggott in Chester Co., PA; died 24 10th mo (December) 1737 in Chester Co., PA (now Cecil Co., MD

Children of John Piggott and Margery Brown:

a. James, born 16 11th mo (January) 1714/15
b. Margery (1), born 30 6th mo (August) 1715; died 8 1st mo (March) 1728/29
c. John, born 18 2nd mo (April) 1717
d. Samuel, born 11 August 1718
e. Elizabeth, born 15 5th mo (July) 1720; md _____ Crompton; died 8 5th mo (July) 1747
f. Abigail, born 30 11th mo (January) 1721/22
g. Susannah, born 13 1st mo (March) 1723/24
h. Jeremiah (1), born 26 6th mo (August) 1725; died a few months after his birth
i. William; born 8 6th mo (August) 1726
j. A son born 10 4th mo (June) 1729; died 16 4th mo (June) 1729
k. Jeremiah (2), born 26 8th mo (October) 1730
l. Benjamin, born 29 9th mo (November) 1732
m. A son born 26 8th mo (October) 1734; died 1 9th mo (November) 1734
n. Margery (2), born 20 12th mo (February) 1735

vi. Daniel, md 4 1st mo (March) 1716/17 Elizabeth Kirk, dau of Alphonsus and Abigail (Sharpley) Kirk of New Castle Co., DE

Children of Daniel Brown and Elizabeth Kirk:

a. Elizabeth, born 22 11th mo (January) 1718/19; md 1742 _____ Haines
b. Rachel, born 18 10th mo (December) 1721
c. Daniel, md 27 10th mo (December) 1759 to Miriam Gregg
d. Jeremiah, md 14 9th mo (November) 1765 to Anna Wilson
e. Timothy, md 26 April 1759 to Mary Jones; died 4 April 1808
f. William, md before February 1758 to Elizabeth Knight, dau of William Knight; died before 17 June 1786 in West Nottingham Twp., Chester Co., PA
g. Abigail, md 8 10th mo (December) 1743 at Nottingham Meeting, East Nottingham Twp., Chester Co., PA William Churchman, son of John and Hannah Seary Churchman, died 14 February 1798 in East Nottingham Twp., Chester Co., PA
h. Judith, md before 4 4th mo (June) 1744 _____ Collett; they were married by a "priest" and were disowned by Friends

LOTS 15 & 34
RANDALL JANNEY

Randall Janney was born at Hanford, Staffordshire, England 17 June 1681, the son of **William Janney** and **Deborah Webb**. He died in Philadelphia 7 10th mo (December) 1715. Randall married in 31 8th mo (October) 1731 at Philadelphia Monthly Meeting to **Frances Righton**, the daughter of **William** and **Sarah Righton**. Frances was buried 17 2nd mo (April) 1714 in Philadelphia.

Randall Janney immigrated to Pennsylvania before 29 December 1699, bringing with him a certificate from his former meeting in England. It is unsure whether his brother, Thomas, traveled with him. **Thomas Janney** was born at Hanford, Staffordshire, England 18 March 1669 and died in Cecil Co., MD about 1750, his will having been probated 22 March 1750/51. In March 1701/02, Randall Janney was a purchaser of 1,000 acres of the "Nottingham Lots." It is doubtful that he actually lived there and still maintain a relationship with the Philadelphia Meeting. On the 1st and 2nd of February 1702, Randall Janney was the purchaser of 1000 acres in two lots of 500 acres from **Jno. Willmer** of London, for £120 to be paid in 2 year after and if not paid, the transaction was voided. This land was located between the Susquehanna and Delaware Rivers and was part of a larger tract of 8,000 acres owned by Jno. Willmer. At the March 1705/06 monthly meeting held in Philadelphia, **Richard Hill** complains that Randall Janney is greatly indebted to him and desires that he may be allowed to sue him.

Child of Randall Janney and his wife Frances Righton:

i. William, born 27 12th mo (January 1704) in Philadelphia, PA; died 25 1st mo (March) 1704/05 in Philadelphia, PA

LOTS 16 & 17
JOHN CHURCHMAN

John Churchman, was baptized [20] February 1664 in Saffron Walden Parish, Essex, England, the son of **Robert** and **Elizabeth (Leader) Churchman**. He died in Nottingham Twp., Chester Co., PA between 7 8th mo (October) 1724, when he wrote his will and 10 May 1725, when his will was probated. Nottingham Meeting records give his death date as in the year 1724 and in the journal of his son, John, is stated that John Churchman, Sr. died in the 10th mo (December) 1724. John married **Hannah Seary**, the daughter of **Thomas** and **Sarah Seary**, 26 8th mo (October) 1696 at Concord Meeting, Chester Co., PA. She was born about 1676 in Oxford, Oxfordshire, England and died 22 November 1759 in East Nottingham Twp., Chester Co., PA. The Searys arrived 8 October 1682 on the "Amity" from Downs, England. Thomas Seary was a farrier and a first purchaser of 500 acres in Oxford Twp., Philadelphia Co.,

PA. He did not live long enough to enjoy his new life in Pennsylvania, dying before 29 4th mo (June) 1683.

In March 1701/02, John Churchman was among the group of land purchasers who purchased into the "Nottingham Lots," with his purchase of 1,000 acres. At what point he cleared and moved to Nottingham is not known, but he is listed as a landowner there in 1722. John Churchman was still "of Chester" when he sold 3 tracts of land, containing 54 acres, to John Linvill for £26 in a deed recorded 30 April 1709. In his will, he leaves 150 acres to his eldest son, George; to son John the plantation that he lived on, containing 70 acres, which had been added to his survey; to son Thomas 250 acres; his sons Edward and William received a tract of land of about 300 acres and to his two daughter Dinah and Susanna, a tract of land surveyed upon Chestnut Hill being about 300 acres. This totals 1,070 acres, the sum of his 1701/02 purchase plus the additional land he purchased later. (Chester Co., PA Will Book A:170)

Children of John Churchman and his wife, Hannah Seary

i. George, born 13 7th mo (September 1697) in Chester Co., PA; died 29 April 1767 in East Nottingham Twp., Chester Co., PA

ii. Dinah, born 7 6th mo (August) 1699 in Chester Co., PA; md (1) 11 2nd mo (April 1728) to **Messer Brown**, son of **William** and **Ann (Mercer) Brown**; md (2) 4 9th mo (November) 1736 **Mordecai James**; died 1 January 1766 in East Nottingham Twp., Chester Co., PA

Children of Messer Brown and Dinah Churchman:

a. John, born 1729 in E. Nottingham Twp., Chester Co., PA; md Jane Pugh

b. David, born 1731; md 3 9th mo (November) 1757 Sarah Brown; died before 1793

iii. Susanna, born 13 7th mo (September) 1701 in Chester Co., PA; md William Brown, son of William and Esther (Yearsley) Brown; died 25 August 1790 in Bel Air, Harford Co., MD. Susanna was an esteemed minister among Friends in Philadelphia, where she and her husband lived, a religious, useful woman in meetings of Discipline. She was an Elder and traveled in the company of other women Friends of the ministry to different parts of the colonies. When her eyesight failed, she continued to show her lively intellectual faculties and show an instructive pattern of meekness, patience and resignation to her fellow members.

iv. John, born 29 8th mo (October) 1703 in Chester Co., PA; died 8 9th mo (November) 1703 in Chester, Chester Co., PA

v. John, born 4 6th mo (August) 1705 in Chester Co., PA; md 27 11th mo (January) 1729 to Margaret Brown, daughter of William and Esther (Baker-Yearsley) Brown; died 24 July 1775 in East Nottingham Hundred, Cecil Co., MD. Margaret Brown was born 13 1st mo (March) 1706/07 and died of cancer 28 July 1770 in East Nottingham Hundred, Cecil Co., MD. After the death of his father, John Churchman, took care of the farm and of his mother. He traveled widely in the ministry as a minister among the Religious Society of Friends, along with his brother in law, William Brown. John Churchman was a self-taught surveyor. He was a farmer when he wasn't traveling in his ministry. From 1750 to the Revolutionary War the Nottingham Minutes recorded John Churchman and William Brown as exercised ministers, well known in America and England. Dinah Brown, Joshua Brown and others assisted in their life's work.

Child of John Churchman and his wife Margaret Brown:

a. George, born 1730 in East Nottingham, Chester Co., PA; md Hannah, dau of Mordecai and Gainor James

vi. Thomas, born 16 11th mo (January) 1707/08 in Chester Co., PA; md (1) 5 4th mo (June) 1745 Katherine Reynolds and October 1770 Katherine Jones; died 8 April 1788 in East Nottingham Twp., Chester Co., PA

Children of Thomas Churchman and Katherine Reynolds:

a. Hannah, md Joseph Gatchell
b. Sarah, md David Gatchell

vii. Miriam, born 25 10th mo (December) 1710; md 27 11th mo (January) 1729/30 to James Brown, son of William and Esther (Yearsley) Brown; died 19 November 1750

viii. Edward, born 14 9th mo (November) 1713 in Chester Co., PA; died in February 1723/24, of the smallpox, in East Nottingham Twp., Chester Co., PA

ix. Sarah, born 17 3rd mo (May) 1716 in Chester Co., PA; md 31 11th mo (January) 1744/45 Joseph Trimble in East Nottingham Twp., Chester Co., PA; died 2 8th mo (October) 1750 in East Nottingham Twp.,

Chester Co., PA. Joseph Trimble was born in Co., Antrim, IRE, the son of William and Mary Trimble.

x. William, born 29 11th mo (January) 1720/21 in Chester Co., PA; md 8 10th mo (December) 1743 Abigail Brown, dau of Daniel and Elizabeth (Kirk) Brown; died 15 April 1798 in E. Nottingham Twp., Chester Co., PA. Abigail died 14 February 1798 in East Nottingham Twp., Chester Co., PA. On 17 December 1743, Friends were appointed to make report that the marriage of William Churchman and Abigail Brown was orderly accomplished.

Children of William Churchman and Abigail Brown:

a. Hannah, born 15 10th mo. (December) 1745 in East Nottingham Twp., Chester Co., PA; died in September 1824 in Little Britain Twp., Lancaster Co., PA
b. John, born 21 10th mo (December) 1747 in East Nottingham Twp., Chester Co., PA; md 23 December 1773 Jane Taylor at Swede's Church, Wilmington, DE
c. Elijah, born 10 December 1749 in East Nottingham Twp., Chester Co., PA; md 1776 to Ann Knight
d. Miriam, born 15 8th mo (October) 1751 in East Nottingham Twp., Chester Co., PA; md 19 June 1777 Isaiah Brown, son John and Hannah (Gatchell) Brown; died 13 April 1825
e. Dinah, born 14 11th mo (November) 1753 in East Nottingham Twp., Chester Co., PA; died 23 March 1827 in Little Britain Twp., Lancaster Co., PA
f. Abigail, born 12 11th mo (November) 1755 in East Nottingham Twp., Chester Co., PA; md Rowland Parry son of David and Elizabeth (Ely) Parry; died 28 August 1829 in Little Britain Twp., Lancaster Co., PA
g. William, born 22 November 1757 in East Nottingham Twp., Chester Co., PA
h. Deborah, born 20 February 1759 in East Nottingham Twp., Chester Co., PA
i. Thomas, born 18 February 1761 in East Nottingham Twp., Chester Co., PA
j. Enoch, born 2 November 1762 in East Nottingham Twp., Chester Co., PA
k. David, born 15 December 1766 in East Nottingham Twp., Chester Co., PA; died 17 June 1850 in the 8th District, Cecil Co., MD

LOTS 23, 28 & 33
WILLIAM BROWN

William Brown, brother to James Brown (Lots 14 & 27), was born 29 1st mo (March) 1658/59 in Wellingborough, Northamptonshire, England and died 23 6th mo (August) 1746 in East Nottingham Twp., Chester Co., PA. He married (1) about 1680 in Northamptonshire, **Dorothy Presland**. She died about 1683 soon after their arrival in the colonies. William next married 1 10th mo (December) 1684 at Chester Meeting **Anne Mercer**, daughter of **Thomas** and **Mary Mercer**. Ann was born 1662 in Andover, Wiltshire, England and died about 1696 in Chester Co., PA. William Brown's third wife was **Catherine Williams**, whom he married in 1699 in Philadelphia, PA. Catherine died about 1708 in Chester Co. and three years later, in the 7th mo (September) 1711, William married a fourth time to **Mary Matthews** in Chester Co., PA.

William Brown, his wife Dorothy and infant son, Joseph, immigrated on the ship "Bristol Factor," Roger Drew, master. William shipped to the colonies items that he thought would help him with the starting of a new life. They included 4 cwt nails, wrought iron, 120 goods cotton, 2 cwt. gunpowder, 1¾ cwt. cheese, 1¼ cwt cordage, 11 cwt. lead shot, 56 lbs. brass manufactured, 28 lbs. wrought pewter, 170 ells English made linen, 2 small saddles, 48 lbs. serges, 2 Spanish cloths, 2 dozen and 4 pair woolen stockings, 1 firkin of butter, ? pt of a chalder grindstone, 2 bags and 1 chest of wearing apparel, 1 lb. English thrown silk, 28 lbs. haberdashery wares, 9 parcels of several sorts of wares valued at £14.0.0.

Joseph Besse listed **William** and **James Brown** as prisoners in North Riding with 126 others about 1670. When he was seven, William remembered being concerned about the loss of property for fines from attending meeting and refusing to swear. He remembered how his father, Richard, had been forced to leave his farm and relocate because of the harsh treatment by his landlord, because he refused to swear that he had paid the rent. But he grew up stong in his faith. Both he and his brother, James, were "ministers" when they settled in America.

William Brown purchased of the "Nottingham Lots," lots 23 and 33 for his use and lot 28 for his son, Mercer, who was still underage when the lots were purchased in 1st mo (March) 1701/02. Tradition tells us that William cut the first tree in the settlement of the "Nottingham Lots" in 1702. Concord Meeting records state that William Brown and his family were in Nottingham as of 2nd (April) 1705, where a meeting had been established at his house. The Browns, both William and James, were noted for their zeal as ministers, as well, as for their enterprise and industry. The mill on North East Creek, known as Hurford's Mill, was built by them. **Joseph Trimble** emigrated from Ireland about 1730, at age 15 and served as a wagoner and farm worker for William Brown until 1741 when he settled on his own farm.

When reading William Brown's will, you find that the Quakers were slave owners in the early years of the founding of Pennsylvania. In his will dated, 23 10th mo (December) 1743 and probated 1 October 1746, William Brown left the bulk of his estate to his son, Samuel, with a small bequest to his son, Thomas of £10 "for which he is indebted to me." He also stated, that his "Negro **Jenny** was to get her freedom from the time of my decease do let her perfectly at liberty from me, my heirs, executors and Administrators & assigns forever. I further bequeath and confirm to my said servant woman that bed and bedding whereon she now like, together with those other small things my wife gave her before her (wife's) decease. I also leave my said Negro Jenny the chest which was **James Jones** and orders her all her wearing apparel." (Chester Co., PA Will Book B:209)

After William Brown's death, his memorial stated: "He was of a loving disposition, a serviceable member and elder in the church being a pattern of plainness and bore the marks of a true Christian."

Child of William Brown and Dorothy Presland:

i. Joseph, born 12 4th mo (June) 1682 in England; md 30 9th mo (November) 1710 Margaret Sinkeler (Sinclair); died 30 December 1715 intestate Chester Co., PA

Children of William Brown and Ann Mercer:

ii. Messer (Mercer), born 27 12th mo (February) 1685/87 in Chester Co., PA; md (1) 12 8th mo (October) 1710 Jane Richards, who died 1727-1728 in East Nottingham Twp., Chester Co., PA and (2) 11 2nd mo (April) 1728 Dinah Churchman, dau of John and Hannah (Seary) Churchman.; died before 6 3rd mo (May) 1732 in East Nottingham Twp., Chester Co., PA. Concord Meeting records state that Jane Richards and Mercer (Messer) Brown were both from the Nottingham meeting.

Children of Messer Brown and Jane Richards:

a. Ann, born 28 5th mo (July 1711) in Nottingham Twp, Chester Co., PA; md 15 10th mo (December) 1730 at East Nottingham Mtg. to Richard Beeson

b. Catherine, born 20 10th mo (December) 1712 in Nottingham Twp, Chester Co., PA; md about 1741-1742 Samuel Wilson

c. Hannah, born 27 12th mo (February) 1714/15 in Nottingham Twp., Chester Co., PA; md (1) William Sheppard and (2) 17 10th mo (December) 1734 at East Nottingham Mtg. to Arthur Barrett; died 5 9th mo (November) 1780 in E. Nottingham Twp., Chester Co., PA. Arthur Barrett was an early settler in Nottingham Twp., Chester County, first marrying in the 5th mo (July) 1705 to Lydia Chambers. In 1739 he was granted a certificate of removal for himself and his family to Hopewell Meeting, VA.

d. Messer, born 11 11th mo (January) 1717/1718; md 14 10th mo (December) 1739 Hannah Slater, dau of George and Sarah Slater; died bef. 14 3rd mo (March) 1795 in East Nottingham Twp., Chester Co., PA

Children of Messer Brown and Hannah Slater:

aa. Eli, born in East Nottingham Twp., PA

ab. Jane, born in East Nottingham Twp., Chester Co., PA; md David Parry son of David and Lydia (Richardson) Parry and was dismissed for being married by a "priest"

ac. George, born 2 8th mo (October) 1740 in East Nottingham Twp., Chester Co. PA

ad. Messer, born 16 3rd mo (May 1743) in East Nottingham Twp., Chester Co., PA

ae. Jesse, born 28 7th mo (September) 1745 in East Nottingham Twp., Chester Co., PA

af. David, born 3 1st mo (March) 1746/47 in East Nottingham Twp., Chester Co., PA

ag. Jehu, born 28 2nd mo (April) 1753 in East Nottingham Twp., Chester Co., PA; md (1) 11 October 1778 in Northeast, Cecil Co., MD Sarah Gartrill, dau of John and Mary (Mercer) Gartrill and (2) aft. October 1816 Rachel ______; died bef 20 March 1840 in Calvert, Cecil Co., MD.

e. Jane, born 11 4th mo (June 1720) in East Nottingham Twp., Chester Co., PA; md 8 2nd mo (April) 1742 in East Nottingham Mtg. James Allen, son of James Allen; died 28 September 1778 in Kennett Twp., Chester Co., PA

Children of James Allen and Jane Brown:

aa. William, born 9 11th mo (January) 1742/43 in West Nottingham Twp., Chester Co., PA; died 6 November 1826

ab. David, born 8 3rd mo (May) 1744 in WestNottingham Twp., Chester Co., PA; died 8 July 1745
ac. Hannah, born 15 7th mo (August) 1747 in West Nottingham Twp., Chester Co., PA;
ad. Mary, born 26 11th mo (January) 1750 in West Nottingham Twp., Chester Co., PA
ae. Jane, born 15 January 1753 in West Nottingham Twp., Chester Co., PA
af. Dinah, born 8 March 1757 in West Nottingham Twp., Chester Co., PA
ag. James, born 9 September 1758 in West Nottingham Twp., Chester Co., PA; died 9 January 1759

f. Mary, born 14 6th mo (August) 1722 in East Nottingham Twp., Chester Co., PA; md 8 2nd mo (April) 1742 William Pugh, son of John and Jane Pugh; died 27 November 1751

Children of William Pugh and Mary Brown:

aa. Jean, born 1 3rd mo (May) 1743
ab. Dinah, born 17 11th mo (January) 1744/45
ac. John, born 9 6th mo (August) 1747
ad. Jesse, born 14 6th mo (August) 1751

Children of Messer Brown and Dinah Churchman, *see also entry under John Churchman*:

a. John, born in 1729 in East Nottingham Twp., Chester Co., PA; md Jane Pugh
b. David, born in 1731; md 3 November 1757 Sarah Brown at East Nottingham Mtg.; died before 1793

iii. Ann, born 1 10th mo (December) 1687 in Chester Co., PA; md (1) John Underhill and (2) 13 9th mo (November) 1707 Robert Dutton at William Brown's house in Nottingham, Chester Co., PA
iv. William, born 21 7th mo (September) 1689 in Chester Co., PA; md in (1) in 1715 Elizabeth Cowgill and (2) in 1721 Margaret Davis
v. John, born 3 5th mo (July) 1691 in Chester Co., PA; died 10 10th mo (December) 1715 in Chester Co., PA
vi. Richard, born 21 1st mo (March) 1692/93 in Chester Co., PA; md (1) in 1717 Hannah Reynolds; (2) 1 12th mo (February) 1730/31 Rachel Beeson; (3) 24 8th mo (October) 1737 Mary Norton

vii. Thomas, born 17 11th mo (January) 1694/95 in Chester Co., PA; md abt 1718-1719 Elinor Cowgill; died 19 12th mo (February) 1746/47 in Chester Co., PA

Children of William Brown and Catherine Williams:

viii. Samuel, born 12 8th mo (October) 1700 in Chester Co., PA; md Elizabeth Harris dau William Harris; died 20 1st mo (March) 1746/47
ix. Hannah, born 31 8th mo (December) 1701
x. Mary, born 29 4th mo (June) 1706 in Chester Co., PA; md 23 January 1723/24 William Reynolds

LOTS 29 & 31
ROBERT DUTTON

The first of the Dutton family to arrive in Pennsylvania was the immigrant **John Dutton** and his wife, **Mary Darlington**. John and Mary Dutton came to the colonies from the parish of Overton in Cheshire, England before 8 October 1682, when John had 500 acres of land laid out for him on the west side of Upland Creek. Tradition has it that John Dutton built his house in the meadow near the creek, but being flooded out a number of times, he moved a few rods back and built another dwelling house on a large rock near a small rivulet. There is no record of the death of John Dutton, but we know that it occurred before 12 September 1694 when his widow, Mary and her second husband, **John Nield**, were granted a Bond bearing date 20 August 1694 by the court held at Chester for the sum of £250. John Nield was the indentured servant of **Robert Taylor**, of Springfield Twp., and had fulfilled his indenture by 12 December 1693. He took Robert Taylor to court for money that was owed him and the Court ordered him paid.

At Orphan's Court held 5 March 1694/95, **William Brown** and **John Baldwin** were called to appear to answer the complaint of **John Dutton**, **Edward Dutton** and **Thomas Dutton**, minor children of John and Mary Dutton. The Court ordered that John Nield and Mary, his wife be given guardianship of the three named children and to allow **Thomas Cartwright** and **Joel Baily** to be held as securities for John and Mary Nield for £250. It was also ordered that the old guardian's account be cleared before the new one took effect.

John Dutton sold Lot 29 to **John White**, who established the Cross Keys tavern near the Brick Meeting House.

Children of John Dutton and Mary Darlington:

i. John Dutton
ii. Thomas Dutton
iii. Edward Dutton

iv. Robert Dutton, died in 1724 when on a trip to Antigua, it being his second trip that year. He married 13 9th mo (November) 1707 Ann Brown, dau of William and Ann (Mercer) Brown, at Nottingham at the home of her father. Robert Dutton was one of the first purchaser of 500 acres of the "Nottingham Lots." He was active in the affairs of the Nottingham Meeting, being an overseer in the place of William Brown and John Churchman from 1710 to 1712. Ann (Brown) Dutton was married a second time 23 November 1736 to John Underhill at the home of her father, William Brown. Those appointed by Nottingham Monthly Meeting to inspect her affairs before the marriage, reported that her former husband's estate had been settle by Law.

Children of Robert Dutton and Ann Brown:

a. Mary Dutton, born 15 8th mo (October) 1708
b. Ann Dutton, born 10 10th mo (December) 1711
c. Robert Dutton, born 26 8th mo (October) 1713
d. Elizabeth Dutton, born 25 1st mo (March) 1722, md 20 April 1742 at Nottingham Mtg. to Joseph England, of Kent Co., MD. Joseph was the son of Lewis England.

LOTS 29 & 31
SAMUEL LITTLER

Samuel Littler was christened 26 March 1665 in Frodsham, Cheshire, England, the son of **William** and **Alice Littler** and died 12 3rd mo (May) 1727 in East Nottingham Twp., Chester Co., PA. He was granted a certificate to Chester Meeting where he married 31 5th mo (July) 1707 **Rachel Minshall**, the daughter of **John Minshall** of Great Britain and was the widow of **Thomas Taylor,** whom she married about 27 10th mo (December) 1700 at Chester Meeting. At the time of her marriage to Samuel Littler, Rachel had two children to her first husband, **Thomas** and **Simon Taylor**. Rachel Minshall was born 30 June 1679 and died 22 July 1762. After the death of Samuel Littler, Rachel married for a third time 3 5th mo (July) 1728 at Nottingham Meeting **Thomas Oldham**.

The approximate arrival date of Samuel Littler to the colonies was about 1699. Soon after his arrival he purchase 500 acres of the "Nottingham Lots" in March 1701/02. The lot was described as beginning at the northern barrens between North East River and Octoraro Creek. In 1722, Samuel Littler "desires the Grant of about 300 acres of Land to the Northward of Nottingham, for settling of his sons, 'tis among the Barrens purchased.'" Further stated in the Early Pennsylvania Land records for Samuel Littler, "He is one of the first settlers and has continued in the interest of this Province against the claims of Maryland; he is recommended by **E. Gatchell**."

Samuel Littler wrote his will 8 May 1722, which was probated 30 May 1727 in Chester Co., PA. He gave his wife 200 acres of land at the north end of the Lot, until son John is of age; his son Joshua to get the remaining when he came of age; son Samuel, when of age, was to get 200 acres that had been purchased from Richard Jones; his son Minshall to get 200 acres on Pidgeon Creek, when of age and daughter Sarah was to get £20 when of age. (Chester Co., PA Will Book A:238)

Rachel Oldham wrote her will 23 3rd mo (May) 1761. In it she gave to her son Simon Taylor, 5 shillings and to son Joshua Littler, also 5 shillings; all the remainder of estate, both real and personal to be shared by her granddaughter, Rachel, wife of **Elisha Brown** and **Thomas Barrett**. (Chester Co. Wills)

Children of Samuel Littler and Rachel Minshall:

i. John Littler, born 28 3rd mo (May) 1708 in Chester Co., PA; md 5 June 1728 at Nottingham Meeting to Mary Ross, dau of Alexander and Katherine (Chambers) Ross; died 30 8th mo (October) 1748 in Frederick Co., VA. Alexander Ross and Katherine Chambers were married in the 2nd or 3rd month of 1706. Alexander was another of the "Stolen Children of Scotland", having been brought to this country by Marius Trent and at Court held in Chester Co., PA 3 October 1693 was sold by indenture to Caleb Pusey for a term of ten years, he having been 11 years old when transported. His term of indenture was completed in 1703. Alexander Ross and family lived at Nottingham from 1718 to 1732 before moving, with Morgan Bryan, Josiah Ballinger, James Wright, Evan Thomas and others, to Opeckon Creek in the Shenandoah Valley of Virginia. The Hopewell meeting house, near Winchester was built on land donated by John Littler.

Children of John Littler and Mary Ross:

a. Samuel, born about 1729
b. Mary, born about 1738
c. John, born about 1740
d. Nathan, born about 1742
e. Sarah, born in 1744
f. Rachel, born about 1746

ii. Joshua Littler, born 10 1st mo (March) 1710/11 in Chester Co., PA; md 9 November 1733 at Nottingham Meeting to Deborah Oldham, dau of Thomas and Susannah (Few) Oldham; died 26 November 1774 in Wilmington, DE

Children of Joshua Littler and Deborah Oldham:

a. Thomas, born 10 10th mo (December) 1734
b. Rachel, born 14 8th mo (October) 1736
c. Susannah, born 5 8th mo (October) 1737

iii. Samuel Littler, born 7 12th mo (February) 1712/13 in Chester Co., PA; md 22 6th mo (August) 1735 at Chester Meeting to Mary Ross

Child of Samuel Littler and Mary Ross:

a. Rachel, born 19 9th mo (November) 1737

iv. Rachel, born 21 8th mo (October) 1715 in Chester Co., PA; died 12 1st mo (March) 1726/27
v. Minshall, born 2 2nd mo (April) 1715 in Chester Co., PA; md 5 11th mo (January) 1739/40 at Newark Mtg to Lydia Woodward; died in 1740 in Wilmington, DE
vi. Sarah, born 24 6th mo (August) 1721 in Chester Co., PA; md 7 October 1742 at Nottingham Meeting to John Pugh, son of John and Jane Pugh of East Nottingham; died 2 6th mo (August) 1743.

Child of John Pugh and Sarah Littler:

a. Joshua, born 25 June 1743 in East Nottingham Twp., Chester Co., PA

LOTS 32 & 35
ANDREW JOB(E)

Tradition tells us that **Andrew Job(e)** was born on board a ship sailing for the Massachusetts Colony about the year 1650, the son of **Andrew Job(e)**. He died 5 June 1722 in Nottingham Twp., Chester Co., PA. It is unsure when he traveled to the Pennsylvania Colony, but it is thought that he was there to greet William Penn when he landed with the "Welcome." Andrew married 3 October 1692 **Elizabeth Vernon**, daughter of **Thomas Vernon**.

On 14 June 1692, Andrew Jobe of Chester, carpenter, purchased a tract of land in Chester, bounded by Chester Creek and the land of **George Churchman**, containing 100 acres, from the heirs of **Thomas Brassey**. In March 1701/02. Andrew Job was a purchaser of 1000 acres of the land grant that became known as the "Nottingham Lots." At what time he made Nottingham his home is not known. But it must have been between the time he was still listed as Andrew Job "of Chester" in a 27 April 1709 deed, in which he sold to **William Pusey**, of Chester, the land that he purchased in 1692 and by 1710 when he established the first tavern in Nottingham on Lot #35 in a small brick house on the property.

In his will, in which Andrew Job wrote 30 March 1722, he gave to his son Jacob, two of the lots where he is now settled and to his son Abraham; the other two, to son Enoch, the tract of land upon Little Elk Creek; to son Thomas, 200 acres of land of the south end of the lot whereon "I" live; to son-in-law John White, £5; to grandchildren, William, John and Mary White, 20 shillings each when 10 years old; to grandson Nathan Job, 40 shillings when 10; to wife Elizabeth, "my plantation whereon I live," during her widowhood and afterwards to younger sons, Caleb and Joshua, they paying to their two younger sisters, Hannah and Patience, £10 each when of age. The will was probated 13 November 1722. (Chester Co., PA Will Book A:140)

Children of Andrew Job and Elizabeth Vernon:

i. Benjamin, born 13 8th mo (October) 1693 in Chester Co., PA; died 1 9th mo (November) 1693 in Chester Co., PA

ii. Jacob, born 3 3rd mo (May) 1694 in Chester Co., PA

iii. Thomas, born 15 9th mo (November) 1695; md 28 8th mo (October) 1725 at Nottingham Mtg to Elizabeth Maxwell, the niece of author, Daniel Defoe. When just eighteen years old and so much in love, Elizabeth contracted to marry without her mother's consent. The engagement was broken and Elizabeth ran away from home and embarked for America. Unable to pay for her passage, she bound herself to the captain and upon arrival in Philadelphia, was sold as an indentured servant to reimburse him the money she owed for her passage. She was purchased by Andrew Job, of Nottingham, who took her to her new home. After serving her indenture for a number of years, she married Thomas Job. Elizabeth wrote to her mother and uncle to let them know of her whereabouts and that she was safe and happily married. Her Uncle Daniel wrote her to let her know of her mother's death and that there was an inheritance from her mother's estate. An inventory was included with the letter, in which is mentioned "two chairs, the wicker seats of which were worn and replaced with wooden ones." One of these chairs had been donated to the Historical Society of Delaware in Wilmington, DE by Joseph Trimble. Elizabeth (Maxwell) Job died 7 September 1782 at the age of 82 and is buried at Brick Meetinghouse Friends Burying ground, Calvert, MD. One of her grandsons, Daniel Defoe Job, spoke of his grandmother as a little, old, yellow looking woman, fond of flowers and retaining her activity of mind and body until her death.

Children of Thomas Job and Elizabeth Maxwell:

a. James, bur 30 1st mo (January) 1803 at Brick Meetinghouse Friends Burying ground
b. Daniel, md 26 10th mo (October) 1758 at East Nottingham Mtg to Mary Brown dau of Samuel and Elizabeth (Harris) Brown

iv. Mary, born 27 1st mo (March) 1696/97 in Chester Co., PA; md 30 8th mo (October) 1717 at Nottingham Meeting to John White, son of William White of New Castle Co., DE, wheelwright

Children of John White and Mary Job:

a. William, born 21 5th mo (July) 1718; md 10 9th mo (November) 1743 at East Nottingham to Sarah Pugh, dau of John and Jane Pugh
b. John, born 13 10th mo (December) 1719
c. Mary, born 20 5th mo (July) 1721
d. Samuel, born 28 11th mo (January) 1722

v. Enoch (1), born 9 7th mo (September) 1698 in Chester Co., PA
vi. Enoch (2), born 7 11th mo (January) 1700/01; md 6 3rd mo (May) 1731 at Nottingham Mtg to Abigail Gatchell, dau of Elisha and Rachel (Wilcox) Gatchell; estate probated 15 12th mo (February) 1731/32
vii. Abraham, born 14 6th mo (August) 1702; md 24 9th mo (November) 1726 at East Nottingham Mtg to Sarah Gatchell, dau of Elisha and Rachel (Wilcox) Gatchell
viii. Caleb, born 26 5th mo (July) 1704
ix. Joshua, born 2 1st mo (March) 1706/07; md 11 1st mo (March) 1730/31 at Nottingham Mtg to Margaret McCoy, dau of Robert McCoy of Milford Hundred, Cecil Co., MD
x. Hannah, born 24 8th mo (October) 1708
xi. Patience, born 2 7th mo (September) 1710; md 21 1st mo (March) 1735/36 at Nottingham Mtg to Robert McCoy, of Orange Co., VA, son of Robert McCoy

LOTS 36 & 37
JOHN BEALS

Little is known of the immigrant, **John Beals**. The first evidence that we have of him in Pennsylvania is at the Chester Monthly Meeting of 1 January 1682/83, in which he stated his intentions for the second time to marry **Mary Clayton**, dau of **William** and **Prudence (Lanckford) Clayton**. Mary

Clayton was born 29 June 1665 and died in 1725 in East Nottingham before that of her husband. John Beals, of Nottingham Twp., wrote his will 11 October 1726. In it he mentions his eldest son, John, giving him a bed and furniture and £5, he to pay to his five children, viz Sarah, John, Thomas, Ann and Phebe, 10 shillings when of age; to daughter, Mary Harrold, £8, she to pay to each of her children, viz: Elizabeth, Rachel, Jonathan and Richard each 10 shillings when of age; to son Jacob £12, he to pay his 4 children, viz John, Jacob, Mary and William 10 shillings each when of age; to daughter Patience Jones, the £8-15 due of a bond of her husband and £5 more for her children, viz: Judith, Mary, Sarah and Charity 10 shillings each, when they come of age. To kinswoman, **Mary Davis**, of Philadelphia, 20 shillings. The will was probated 17 December 1726. (Chester Co., PA Will Book A:206)

John Beals was a purchaser of 1000 acres of the "Nottingham Lots" in March 1701/02. He moved his family from Aston Twp., Chester Co., PA to Nottingham about the year 1704.

Children of John Beals and Mary Clayton:

i. John, yeoman, born 20 March 1685/86 in Chester Co., PA; died before 1745 Frederick Co., VA; md 14 November 1711 at Chester Mtg. Sarah Bowater, dau of Thomas and Sarah (Edge) Bowater of Chester Creek, PA

Children of John Beals and Sarah Bowater:

a. Sarah, born 29 July 1713 in Chester Co., PA; md _____ Miles. At Concord Meeting 29 3rd mo (May) 1733. Sarah made an acknowledgment for being married by a "priest" and disorderly conversation some years past when she was living in Chester. Her father requested a certificate for her to Nottingham, she being removed to Monocasy (Virginia), which is in the verge of Nottingham meeting.
b. John, born 17 2nd mo (April) 1717 in Chester Co., PA
c. Thomas, born 14 1st mo (March) 1719/20 in Chester Co., PA

ii. William, born 1 2nd mo (April 1687) in Chester Co., PA; md 26 4th mo (June 1712) at Nottingham Mtg to Rebeckah Chambers, dau of John Chambers of Chichester

Child of William Beals and Rebeckah Chambers:

a. Lydia, born 1 6th mo (August) 1719 in Chester Co., PA

iii. Jacob, born 28 7th mo (September) 1689 in Chester Co., PA; md 20 4th mo (June) 1714 at Nottingham Mtg to Mary Brooksby, dau of John Brooksby of the Province of Maryland. Mary died at Warrington, York Co., PA 3 11th mo (November) 1763 at age 68 years.

Children of Jacob Beals and Mary Brooksby:

a. John, born 11 7th mo (September) 1715
b. Jacob, born 18 7th mo (September) 1717
c. Mary, born 15 9th mo (November) 1719
d. William, born 16 9th mo (November) 1721

iv. Mary, born 24 4th mo (June) 1692 in Chester Co., PA; md 1 4th mo (June) 1710 at Chester Mtg to Richard Harrold

Children of Richard Harrold and Mary Beals:

a. Elizabeth, born 10 3rd mo (May) 1711; md 18 June 1730 at the house of Josiah Ballengar at Monocasy to Thomas Mills, son of John Mills of Monocasy near the Potomac River
b. Mary (1), born 28 1st mo (March) 1713/14
c. John, born 21 10th mo (December) 1714
d. Jonathan, born 20 11th mo (January) 1717/18
e. Mary (2), 19 9th mo (November) 1718
f. Rachel, 9 2nd mo (April) 1721
g. Richard

v. Patience Beals, born 15 4th mo (June) 1695 in Chester Co., PA; md 20 4th mo (June) 1717 at Nottingham Mtg to Joseph Jones, maulster, of Nottingham Twp., son of John Jones of Worstershire, England

Children of Joseph Jones and Patience Beals:

a. Judith, born 1 5th mo (July) 1718
b. Mary, born 2 4th mo (June) 1720
c. Sarah
d. Charity, born 27 8th mo (October) 1725

Arthur Barrett and his wife, **Lydia Chambers** settled in Nottingham before 1718. He was listed on the 1718 tax list for East Nottingham. He was granted a certificate to Hopewell Meeting in Virginia 19 3rd mo (May) 1739 from Nottingham Meeting.

Children of Arthur Barrett and Lydia Chambers:

i. John, born 23 10th mo (December) 1707; md 11 10th mo (December) 1735 at East Nottingham Mtg to Mary Pugh, dau of John Pugh of EAST Nottingham

ii. Arthur Barrett, born 7 11th mo (January) 1709; md (1) 17 10th mo (December) 1734 at East Nottingham Mtg. to Hannah Brown, dau of Mercer (Messer) and Jane (Richards) Brown; (2) ______ Sheperd

iii. Thomas, born 16 1st mo (March) 1711/12; died 19 2nd mo (February) 1782; md 29 9th mo (November) 1739 to Hannah Oldham, dau of Thomas Oldham

Children of Thomas Barratt and Hannah Oldham:

a. Rebekah, born 7 8th mo (October) 1740
b. Arthur, born 10 7th mo (September) 1742
c. Rachel, born 12 9th mo (November) 1744; md John Pugh
d. Thomas, born 23 11th mo (January) 1746
e. Lydia, born 30 7th mo (September) 1749
f. Susanna, born 30 7th mo (July) 1752
g. William, born 4 4th mo (April) 1755
h. Mary, born 16 12th mo (December) 1756; died 8 April 1817 at East Nottingham
i. Deborah, born 16 12th mo (December) 1756 (twin to Mary)
j. Hannah, born 5 5th mo (May) 1759
k. Joseph, born 15 7th mo (July) 1766; died 19 6th mo (June) 1782

iv. William, born 15 2nd mo (April) 1713

v. Richard, born 20 10th mo (December) 1717

Benjamin Chandlee was born 1685 in Ireland, the son of **William** and **Joanna Chandlee** of Kilmore, co. Kildare and died 18 September 1745 in Wilmington, DE. He came to Philadelphia with a certificate from Edenderry Meeting, Kings Co. [now Co. Offaly], about 1701. He married 25 3rd mo (May) 1710 to **Sarah Cottey**, the daughter of **Abel** and **Mary Cottey**. Benjamin Chandlee is listed as a "miller" at the time of his marriage. Benjamin indentured himself to Abel Cottey, the first clockmaker in Philadelphia, to learn the clock and instrument making business. In 1706, Abel Cottey purchased 400 acres of land from Randall Janney, a first purchaser in the "Nottingham Lots" and another small piece of land near the Brick Meetinghouse. When Abel Cottey died in 1711, he left the smaller property in Nottingham to his wife, Mary, and she gave it to Benjamin and Sarah. The land that he bought of Randall Janney, Abel Cottey gave to them upon their marriage. At Philadelphia Meeting 26 7th mo (September) 1712, Benjamin Chandlee asks for a certificate to Nottingham intending to remove there with his family. Benjamin is known to have made 40 clocks in the 30 years that he lived at Nottingham. He also did ironwork for his neighbors recognizing a need for this service. In 1741, he and Sarah moved to Wilmington, DE to live leaving Benjamin Chandlee, Jr., at age 18, to continue with the making of surveyors' instruments and clocks in the Nottingham area. The original mill where the Chandlee clocks were made is no longer standing, although his home, that he built of stone, is.

Children of Benjamin Chandlee and Sarah Cottey:

i. Mary, born 1711; md Neal McCaskey, of Fawn Twp., York Co., PA
ii. Cottey, born ca. 1713; died 9 10th mo (October) 1807, bur at Friends Graveyard at East Nottingham
iii. Hannah, born 24 1st mo (March) 1717/18
iv. William, md 10 7th mo (September) 1748 to Mary Elgar, dau of Joseph and Mary Elgar; died 2 1st mo (January) 1806 and is buried at Friends Graveyard at Middletown
v. Benjamin, md 17 12th mo 1749 at Newark Mtg to Mary Folwell, dau of Edward Folwell of Wilmington, DE; died 18 9th mo (September) 1791 or 1794

Children of Benjamin Chandlee and Mary Folwell:

a. Goldsmith Chandlee, born 18 7th mo (July) 1751; md (1) 15 February 1776 at Hopewell Meeting, VA to Ann White; (2) 28 October 178 Nottingham Mtg. to Hannah Yarnall; (3) 12 June 1811 at Smith Creek, Shenandoah, VA to Eunice Rogers; died 4 March 1821 in Winchester, VA
b. Sarah, born 10 4th mo (April) 1753; md Abner Kirk; died 5 August 1808
c. Ellis, born 11 6th mo (June) 1755; md 1 May 1792 to Elizabeth Giles Oldham; died 28 June 1816 in Nottingham
d. John, born 10 7th mo (July) 1757; md 3 times; died 12 May 1813 in Nottingham

e. Isaac, born 12 9th mo (September) 1760; died 10 December 1819 in Nottingham

vi. Abel, born 1 12th mo (February) 1726; died in 1807 at Nottingham, PA

Aaron Coppock was born 25 10th mo (December) 1662 in Cheshire and died 10 10th mo (December) 1725 at Nottingham, Chester Co., PA. Aaron married 30 9th mo (November) at Chichester Meeting to **Miriam Short**, the sister to **Joel Baily's** wife and widow of **William White**. She was married first to **George Thompson.**

Aaron Coppock wrote his will 3 October 1726 and it was probated 17 December 1726. Bequests were given to son John, the plantation "where I live", containing 300-400 acres, when he comes of age, subject to wife's return; daughters Lydia and Miriam Coppock, Sarah Frazer, Martha Robinson and Mary Sinclair, 5 shillings each; to son-in-law Ralph Thompson, money that is "due me", 40 shillings; son-in-law Samuel White and daughter-in-law Elizabeth White, 5 shillings each. (Chester Co., PA Will Book A:205)

Child of George Thompson and Miriam Short:

i. Ralph, born ca. 1683

Children of William White and Miriam Short:

ii. John, of Nottingham, husbandman; md 21 8th mo (October) 1717 to Mary Job, dau of Andrew and Elizabeth (Vernon) Job
iii. Samuel, md 21 2nd mo (April) 1726 to Hannah Piggott
iv. Elizabeth

Children of Aaron Coppock and Miriam Short:

v. John, born abt 1719; md 16 1st mo (March) 1731/32 at W. Nottingham Mtg to Margaret Coulson, dau of Joseph and Margaret Coulson; died 18 5th mo (May) 1789, aged 80 years

Children of John Coppock and Margaret Coulson:

a. John, born 18 9th mo (November) 1736
b. Ann, born 24 6th mo (August) 1738
c. Margaret, born 24 7th mo (September) 1740
d. Joseph, born 24 2nd mo (April) 1742
e. Thomas, born 12 2nd mo (April) 1744

f. Samuel, born 3 11th mo (January) 1748

vi. Miriam, md 12 8th mo (October) 1727 at W. Nottingham Mtg to Richard Jones, of Nottingham
vii. Lydia
viii. Sarah, md ______ Frazer
ix. Martha, md ______ Robinson
x. Mary, md ______ Sinclair

Elisha Gatchell was born about 1682 in Marblehead, Massachusetts, the son of **Jeremiah** and **Elizabeth (Boude) Gatchell** and died in the winter of 1753/54 in Nottingham. He settled in Philadelphia about 1704. Elisha was married to **Rachel Wilcox** before they signed a release of real estate on 27 6th mo (August) 1706. Rachel was the daughter of **Barnabas** and **Sarah Wilcox** of Radnor Meeting. The move to Nottingham for Elisha and Rachel occurred in 1715. At the time of his moving to Nottingham, Elisha was not a Quaker. It wasn't until 1722 that he attended a meeting and "desired to be joined with Friends." They took the matter under consideration and granted his wish to join the meeting. Elisha Gatchell was a Justice of the Peace and very involved in the border dispute between Pennsylvania and Maryland. Rachel Gatchell wrote her will 17 February 1756, which was probated 26 August 1760. In it she gave her son Elisha, and daughters Elizabeth Mitchell, Abigail Price, Esther Brown, Hannah Brown and Ann Kirk, each £20; granddaughter, Sarah, daughter of Joshua Brown, one heifer; grandson Elisha Price, a Mulatto boy until he is 30 years old and he is to be taught to read and write; Hannah Brown also received the interest on her husband's bond; Joshua Brown to receive £10 and Ann Kirk also received the interest on her husband, Timothy's bond. (Chester Co., PA Wills)

Children of Elisha Gatchell and Rachell Wilcox:

i. Sarah, md 24 9th mo (November) 1726 at Nottingham Mtg to Abraham Job, son of Andrew and Elizabeth (Vernon) Job
ii. Elizabeth, md (1) 24 9th mo (November) 1726 at Nottingham Mtg to Thomas Hughes; (2) Edward Mitchell
iii. Abigail, md (1) 24 10th mo (December) 1727 to Enoch Job, son of Andrew and Elizabeth (Vernon) Job; (2) John Price
iv. Elisha, born 1 2nd mo (April) 1711; died in 1789; md (1) 3 8th mo (August) 1733 to Mary Worley, dau of Henry and Anne (Stone) Worley; (2) Anne ______
v. Hannah, died bef 1767; md 15 10th mo (December) 1736 to Joshua Brown, son of Jeremiah and Mary Brown. Joshua Brown md (2) Zillah Maule, widow of Thomas

Child of Joshua Brown and Hannah Gatchell

a. Hannah, md in 1776 her stepbrother **Daniel Maule**, son of **Thomas** and **Zillah Maule**

vi. Esther, md 31 3rd mo (May) 1739 to Jeremiah Brown, son of Jeremiah and Mary (Cole) Brown
vii. Anne, md 29 8th mo (October) 1741 to Timothy Kirk, son of Roger and Elizabeth (Richards) Kirk; died 8 1st mo 1766

James King was born in 1673 and died in 1768 in Little Britain Twp., Lancaster Co., PA. He married 28 2nd mo (April) 1709 at Concord Mtg to **Isabel Pennell**. James King was one of the organizers of West Nottingham Meeting. Sometime before 1733, James and Isabel moved to Little Britain in the Conowingo Valley in southern Lancaster Co., PA, where James King was granted 500 acres 14 January 1735.

Children of James King and Isabel Pennell:

i. Mary, born 19 12th mo (February) 1710; died 2 3rd mo (March) 1788
ii. Margaret, born 20 10th mo (December) 1712; md 23 11th mo (January) 1739 to Richard Sidwell, son of Hugh and Anne Sidwell
iii. Michael, born 30 10th mo (December) 1714; died 1770, leaving no direct heirs. He gave the land for the Penn Hill Meeting House in Fulton Twp., Lancaster Co., PA
iv. Thomas, born 28 7th mo 1716; md 11 12th mo (December) 1755 at Little Britain Mtg. to Ann Coppock, dau of John and Margaret Coppock
v. Jane, born 19 9th mo (November) 1718; died 12 9th mo (September) 1797
vi. Vincent, born 5 5th mo (July) 1720; md 12 12th mo 1770 to Mary Brown, dau of Joshua and Hannah (Gatchell) Brown; died 14 10th mo (December) 1801
vii. Hannah, born 3 7th mo (September) 1722

Hugh Sidwell was born 7 September 1662 in Letcomb Regis, Berkshire, England the son of **Richard** and **Frances (West) Sidwell** and died in West Nottingham Twp., Chester Co., PA in 1729. Hugh and his wife, **Elizabeth Goulding** migrated from Berkshire and settled in West Nottingham about 1715.

Children of Hugh Sidwell and Elizabeth Goulding:

i. Richard, born 9 April 1704 in Letcomb Regis, Berkshire, England; md 23 11th mo (January) 1739 at West Nottingham Mtg to Margaret

King, dau of James and Isabel (Pennell) King; died 10 9th mo (November) 1740

ii. John

iii. Hugh, born in Letcomb Regis, Berkshire; md Ann Hayes; died 8 September 1840

Children of Hugh Sidwell and Ann Hayes:

a. Henry, born 2 4th mo June 1720; md 12 9th mo 1764 at West Nottingham Mtg. to Margaret Hagan, dau of Catherine Hagan of Baltimore Co., MD

b. Richard, born 11 12th mo (February) 1723; md 4 8th (October) at East Nottingham to Ann Job, dau of Thomas Job & Elizabeth Maxwell; died 10 November 1815

c. Hugh, born 25 7th mo (September) 1725

d. Abraham, born 11 2nd mo (April) 1727; md 5 5th mo (July) 1756 at West Nottingham Mtg to Charity Harris, dau of John and Phebe Harris

e. Isaac, born 5 11th mo (January) 1729; md 2 10th mo (October) 1756 at West Nottingham Mtg to Anne Brown, dau of Thomas and Ellen Brown

f. Jacob, born 15 5th mo (July) 1732; died 28 September 1818 at the Hermitage in West Nottingham Twp., Chester Co., PA of dysentery

g. Ann, born 11 6th mo 1734; md (1) 11 5th mo (July) 1757 at W. Nottingham to Jeremiah Sergent; (2) Benjamin Wilson; died in December 1805 in West Nottingham Twp., Chester Co., PA

h. Joseph, born 3 11th mo (January) 1736; md 30 9th mo (September) to Rachel Midcalf, dau of James and Margaret Midcalf of Little Britain Twp., Lancaster Co.,

i. Mary, born 2 8th mo (October) 1739

NOTTINGHAM LOTS TIMELINE

1631 The colony of Maryland was named for Charles I wife, Queen Henrietta Maria.

1652 After several years of searching George Fox gathered the many groups of seekers into the group known as the Society of Friends of the Truth.

1674 James II gave Lords Berkley and Carteret land in New Jersey and New York. Lord Berkley, wishing to pay for his new house in London convinced Edward Byllinge to buy West Jersey. Byllinge had no money and asked John Fenwick to purchase it, which Fenwick did for £1,000 about $1,000,000 in today's dollars. A dispute arose over this deal and William Penn was called in to settle it. Penn became aware of the land for settlement between Maryland and Connecticut. Since Penn's father, a famous English admiral, Sir William Penn had spent £16,000 for "dieting" his sailors in the Royal Navy, King Charles II, out of "regard to the memorie and meritts of his late father," agreed to the younger Penn's request to the King to grant him land in the territory between Lord Baltimore's province of Maryland and the Duke of York's province of New York.

1681 On June 24, 1680, Penn asked King Charles II (1660-1685) for a charter for land in America. The only available tract in eastern North America lay west of New Jersey, north of Maryland, and south of New York, an area that England had conquered from the Dutch in 1664 and which the King had given to his brother James, the Duke of York, later King James II. After appropriate discussions the King granted the thirty-seven-year-old Penn's request on March 4, 1681.

1682 In 1682, the Duke of York deeded to Penn his claim to the three lower counties on the Delaware Bay, which are now the state of Delaware.

William Penn, the Proprietor, arrived in America on the "Welcome" at the end of October, 1682. The charters granted to Penn and to Lord Baltimore were hopelessly in conflict. Lord Baltimore asserted that his charter properly included Delaware, and he also claimed so large a portion of southern Pennsylvania that the site chosen for Philadelphia would have gone to Maryland.

1683 Consistent with the Society of Friends' (Quakers) belief that all people are children of God and should be considered equals, William Penn attempted to treat Native Americans fairly. Although King Charles II had granted to Penn in 1681 the land the crown called "Pennsylvania," Penn also purchased it from the indigenous people, acknowledging them as the rightful owners. He made his first purchase in 1682 and continued this practice in the following years. Many were for small tracts, some overlapping others. Penn purchased two plots of land from the Indians that probably were a part of the Nottingham Lots in 1683.

1684 Penn learned that Lord Baltimore was on his way back to England and would try to persuade the King to give Maryland the lands that were in dispute between the two colonies. Penn knew that he must also go back if he were not to lose a large portion of his land. In August of 1684 he hurriedly left for England to protect his colony's interests. He was not to return to the colony for fifteen years. The boundary quarrel dragged on interminably, and although Penn was able to prevent a transfer of the disputed lands to Maryland, he did not succeed in gaining a clear title to them himself.

1688 As a result of the English Revolution of 1688, which overthrew King James II, Penn was deprived of his province from 1692 until 1694.

1701 In December 1699, the Proprietor again visited Pennsylvania. During the period after the accession of William and Mary in England, Lord Baltimore fell into disfavor. William Penn pushed his settlements southward into George Talbot's Susquehanna Manor grant and here laid out the 37 lots of 500 acres each under the name of "Nottingham." With a small band of settlers, mostly Quakers and friends whom he had known in England, William Penn set out from Chester on an exploratory trip from the mouth of the Octoraro toward the tide water of the Chesapeake Bay. Here he selected a site "where water descended in all directions" and granted the 40 acres of ground to his Quaker followers and their successors for "a Meeting house and Burial Yard, forever."

The Charter of Privileges was the adopted as a new frame of government for the colony in October 1701. The bell cast in 1751 to mark the fiftieth anniversary of the Charter of Privileges was engraved with the words, "Proclaim liberty throughout the land unto all the inhabitants thereof," from the Book of Leviticus, Chapter 25, and Verse 10. Today known as the Liberty Bell, it is housed Independence National Historic Park in Philadelphia. A determined movement to place Pennsylvania under the direct control of the Crown was at work in Parliament. Penn, again, had to hurry back to England. He sailed in November 1701.

Brothers William and James Brown were said to be the first of the settlers of the 18,000 acres of 35 lots that were established between the Naaman's and "Otterario" Creeks. Lord Talbot had surveyed his Susquehanna Manor between the mouths of these two creeks, which Lord Baltimore considered the northern limits of Maryland. For the most part they were 500 acre to 1,000-acre plots, located north of this boundary. The settlers paid £8 within one year for every 100 acres. They were to pay one shilling or two bushels of good wheat yearly in quit rent. Andrew Job, a settler, had been a sheriff in Chester County and he convinced others to come settle in the area. Many came from Chichester and surrounding areas including: Joel Baily, John Beales, Edward Beeson, John Churchman, James Cooper, Robert Dutton, Randal Janney, Samuel Littler, and Henry Reynolds. Some of families had roots in New Jersey, including the Coopers, Browns, Haines and Reynolds. They came because the tall timber of fine oak and other wood indicated this was good farmland. Meeting for Worship was held in their homes. John Guest, Cornelius & Ebenezer Empson, and John Richardson were speculators who never settled in the area.

1702 The first permanent settlements in this neighborhood were made in 1702 when two brothers, James and William Brown, Andrew Job, John Churchman, Messer Brown, Jeremiah Brown and a few others, on pack horses from New Castle (which was then next to New York in commerce and population) came into the wilderness to make themselves a home. The brothers Brown, like their father, were ministers of the gospel and in 1704 a meeting was organized at the house of James, which was origin of the Quaker congregation of East Nottingham. Edward Shipppen, Thomas Story, James Logan, and Henry Hollingsworth laid out the plots. Hollingsworth was the surveyor.

1705 Concord Meeting recognized the Friends' meeting on the Nottingham Lots as an allowed meeting under its care.

1709 With an interpreter, Thomas Chalkley led an expedition from Nottingham Meeting on a religious visit to the Seneca and Shawansee Indians at Conestoga. His zeal equaled by his meekness touched their hearts and he was kindly received. One tribe was governed by an 'empress' whose advice the Indians sought before they consented to hold a meeting. When the surprised Quakers questioned this, the Indians replied that, "some women are wiser than some men."

1710 The first tavern was established about 1710, on Lot 35 of the Nottingham Lots by Andrew Job. Job's son, Thomas, married Elizabeth Maxwell, niece of Daniel Defoe, author of *Robinson Crusoe.*

1711 Benjamin Chandlee, emigrated from Ireland arriving in Philadelphia in 1701. Having learned the trade of clockmaker from Abel Cottey, he married Cottey's daughter, Sarah, in 1710 and the couple located at Nottingham after Abel Cottey's death in 1722. Three sons and three daughters were born to the Chandlees. Benjamin, Jr. born in 1723 attained eminence in the manufacture of scientific, mathematical and chemical instruments but probably best known in Cecil County for the clocks that bear his name. His sons, Isaac and Ellis, carried on the firm of Chandlee & Sons, with equal success after their father's death until Isaac died on December 10, 1813.

1715 Newark Meeting was the caretaker of the Nottingham Meeting. A school may have been established at Nottingham. Two log-schools were erected in the area, one near the meetinghouse and the other near Stubb's mill.

The Maryland Legislature passed a law that all servants were to give a three-month notice to their employers and filed in the courthouse. Thus they could obtain passes to move freely. They also made it illegal to help anyone, but a freeman, to be transported. This usually meant whites, but it led into illegally moving the run away slaves.

1718 New Garden Meeting became the overseeing meeting. William Penn died on July 30, 1718, at the age of seventy-three.

1719 West Nottingham Meeting was established by James King and James Harris. Roger Kirk, a weaver, who came to America from Ireland in 1712 and purchased property after death of James Brown in 1714 and built his home on Lot 27.

1724 An impressive two and one-half storied brick structure was built, known as Brick Meeting House, and is the 8th oldest church in Maryland. Slate for the roof was found along the Octorara.

1730 The first West Nottingham Meeting House was built.

1739 John Day established his tanyard about 1739.

1740 Joseph England settled on land Penn had granted to James Parke in 1681. Joseph England's brother settled at Principo Furnace.

Gilbert Tennent (1703-1764), a Presbyterian leader of the Great Awakening in the Middle Colonies. Upon George Whitefield's departure from the colonies in 1741, he deputized his friend Tennent to come from New Jersey to New England to "blow up the divine fire lately kindled there." Despite being ridiculed as "an awkward and ridiculous Ape of Whitefield," Tennent managed to keep the revival going until 1742.

In this famous sermon, preached at Nottingham, Pennsylvania, in 1740, Tennent lashed opponents who had reservations about the theology of the new birth as "Pharisee-Shepherds" who "with the Craft of Foxes . . . did not forget to breathe the Cruelty of Wolves in a malicious Aspersing of the Person of Christ."

1744 The front portion of Cross Keys Tavern was built by Thomas Hughes and was halfway point between Baltimore and Philadelphia on the old stage post road.

1745 John Churchman, the son of John Churchman, the original settler, was distinguished for his piety and his ability as a preacher. He built a brick house on the family lot and had the date 1745 placed on the brickwork on the east end. George Churchman, the younger John Churchman's son, was founder of Westtown School, the first Quaker boarding school in America.

1748 The Meeting House burned and was rebuilt with a stone addition. Elisha Rowls' father was a carpenter on this building.

1750 William Brown and brother-in-law John Churchman were recognized ministers among Friends and traveled widely, including to Great Britain. This was probably the peak year for the importance of East Nottingham Meeting. The minutes reflect much tale bearing and worrying about the fornication of Friends while not spending much commentary on issues, such as the school and the later use of the Meeting House as a hospital during the Revolution.

1760 The slavery issue was mentioned in the minutes. By this time most Friends had agreed that slavery was wrong, but a few continued to hold slaves and were censored by their meetings. John White and Benjamin Chandlee gave manumission papers to their slaves.

1762 A coeducational school for the poor of the area including the local "Negroes" was established. It had trouble with funding and did not last too long.

1763 Charles Mason and Jeremiah Dixon begin a survey for the Royal Society to establish the boundaries of the lands of the Penn family and those of the Calverts. The survey, completed in 1769 provided that 16,700 acres of the Nottingham Lots belonged to Maryland, while only 1,300 acres lay within the limits of Pennsylvania. Mason and Dixon spent their winters in the home of the Quaker family of John Harlan. The survey was completed in 1768.

1765 John, Thomas and Richard Penn, heirs of William Penn, deeded title to the Friends, who had held the Meeting House only by verbal declaration. William Penn had "set apart and dedicated forty acres of land to them and their successors forever, for the combined purpose of public worship, the right of burial and the privilege of education."

1780 A new school was erected on the meeting grounds.

1782 Lafayette used the grounds for camping on their way to Yorktown, Virginia.

1788 A petition was presented to the Assembly of Maryland to confirm the titles of the Nottingham Lots residents. Pennsylvania had George Churchman resurvey the northern ends to grant patents.

1793 Because Quakers thought tombstones showy and worldly, John Chandlee was not permitted to erect a stone for his wife, Sara, when she died in 1793. However, he had one carved anyway and stored in the gallery of the meetinghouse. Ultimately, enough of the dissenters had passed on to their reward and he was allowed to erect the tombstone upside down so no one could read the inscription.

1810 The Meeting House burned again. It is said one poplar tree furnished the wood for the benches in the Meeting House.

1811 West Nottingham Meeting built a new meetinghouse. Not wishing to waste anything, the old meetinghouse was purchased by carpenter, Benjamin Reynolds and moved into Rising Sun. He placed it on a lot near his brick house and used it for his shop and stable.

1818 Nottingham Quarter chose to leave Western Quarter of Philadelphia Yearly Meeting and join Baltimore Yearly Meeting.

The Reynolds family had settled the village of Summer Hill and it is said that Israel Reynolds decided to change the name to Rising Sun. Later Eli Reynolds had a drug store near this place.

1830 Before the free schools were established in Cecil County in 1859, several schools were started with land donated by Friends. One examples is the school in Rising Sun, started in 1830 on land donated by Jacob Reynolds.

1847 James Trimble, son of Joseph, gave land from his farm for Rosebank Cemetery and planted boxwood in the area. He was proud of the fact that he knew the botanical names of plants native to Chester and Cecil County.

1853 White Oak School was established when Amassa Churchman conveyed ½ acre to Joseph Harris, Mark Brown and William Kirk. It burned in 1939.

1854 The first school in Colora was Waring's Friends School conducted in William Waring's home. The school continued through 1908.

1876 A Friends Normal School was started in Rising Sun by George P. Passmore.

1890 The first public school was established. A school was started in the Blue Ball area, near the Kirk's Mill on the Little North East Creek, on land donated by Samuel M. Kirk with his wife Victoria involved. Teachers included Ruth Sidwell, Lira White, Margaret Wiley, and Harriet Gatchell. Class size ranged between 40-50 students.

1892 Dr. L. R. Kirk, a graduate of Jefferson Medical College in Philadelphia (class of 1853), sold drugs in a store founded in 1868 in Rising Sun. Items for sale included KIRK'S FAMILY COUGH SYRUP and GILT & EDGE HORSE & CATTLE POWER.

1901 A celebration for the Bicentennial of the founding of the Nottingham Lots was held with about 3,500 participants. It was estimated that 5,000 might have attended had it not been for the news of the assassination of President McKinley that morning of September 14, 1901.

1906 The first agriculture school in Maryland was established next to the East Nottingham Meeting House. This was the first school for higher education in the area. This building was later replaced by an elementary school in the grove north west of the meetinghouse.

1913 John Haines butchered an 800-pound pig, but this record was soon captured by Luke Brown with a 900-pound pig.

SOURCES

Gyles, Anne Thompson. *History of Northeast Maryland and Vicinity.* January 1993.

Havard, Ernest A. *Cecil County Maryland Public Schools: 1850-1958.* Maryland: Students of Cecil Vocational Technical Printing Department, 1970.

"Chandlee Family" a typewritten copy of 1941.

Hubis, Frances M. "Brick Meeting House—Calvert Area." In *300th Anniversary Commemorative Booklet: Historical Sketches and Pictures of Cecil County, Maryland.* edited by Samuel Johnon and Edward D.E. Rollins. Elkton, MD:Cecil Historical Society of Cecil County, 1974.

DARLINGTON

The original Friends Meeting in Harford County was Bush River (1722-1813), which has completely disappeared from the Edgewood/Abingdon area off of Route 7 at the end of Route 136. There is speculation it is at the present sight of a dump. Kirk Brown related that Bush River spun off of West River Meeting in Ann Arundel County, the original Baltimore Yearly Meeting. In 1672 George Fox visited West River along with Josiah Coale and Thomas Thurnston, who arrived about 1658. In 1669 Thomas Thurnston purchased a large tract on Delph Creek in Bush River Neck. Thurnston was elected to the Maryland Assembly in 1688 & 1690 and was disowned by Friends for accepting military appointments. Bush River and Nottingham made up a monthly meeting. At one time, Deer Creek was a combination of Broad Creek Meeting, founded in 1828, and Fawn Grove Meeting, which was active from 1763 until mid-1900s. The existing frame Fawn Meeting House was built in 1878, on Deer Creek. There was concern about the building at Broad Creek, built in 1833, because people seemed to continue to build fires in the meetinghouse.

Edward Plumstead offered to remove it and reconstruct it on his property. He had numbered all parts and stored it in his barn. Unfortunately his barn burned down with the meetinghouse stored inside. The burial ground has tombstones marking the remains of members of the following families: Baily, Bell, Brannen, Crawford, Guifoil, Huff, Pyle, Reed, Scarboro, Somers, Stacks, Stokes, Warner, Wendt, and Williamson.

Deer Creek Meeting today. *Photo by Gail Pietrzyk.*

Deer Creek records date to 1736 and the Meeting may have built as early as 1737. The stone meetinghouse was erected about 1760, a year after they were recognized as a monthly meeting. They split in 1828, forming Orthodox and Hicksite branches, which merged 1949. When they united the newer house, or Orthodox Meeting, was sold and became an apartment house. In 2001, they doubled the size of their meetinghouse with a kitchen and classroom space. Fawn Meetinghouse was sold to another denomination, possibly the Nazarenes. London Grove named a committee to oversee the site and construction of the original Fawn Meeting House.

This meeting found the Susquehanna River to be a major obstacle to get to Western Quarterly Meetings. In 1761, they transferred to West River Quarterly Meeting. By 1819, they rejoined Nottingham Quarter, but the minutes reflect the difficulty of crossing the river or outbreaks of small pox and other obstacles prevented attendance at Quarterly Meetings. Finally in the 1990s, Deer Creek Friends Meeting chose to be an independent meeting.

DRUMORE

Friends settled the area starting about 1795, and petitioned Little Britain Monthly Meeting about 1811 to establish a meeting in Drumore. In 1812 the indulged meeting was held in David Parry's schoolhouse. By 1815, Parry requested advice on building a meetinghouse. It was decided to build a house 30 x 22 1/2 feet Jacob and Joyce Shoemaker gave the land for the meeting house for $1. The committee comprised David Parry, Joseph Stubbs and Samuel Smith. On 10 Eighth month 1816 it was reported that regular meetings were being held and the stone meeting house was built. This meeting was laid down in 1936.

Interior of Drumore Meeting. *Photo by Gail Pietrzyk.*

EAST BRITAIN

On 19 Fifth month 1849 an indulged meeting was held in Ashville. A brick meetinghouse was built on 1 1/2 acres for $40. This was an active Underground

Railroad area. By 1868 minutes record the decision to sell the property. In 1877 Ashville Presbyterian Church purchased it. The building remains as a chapel and has been used by many different churches.

BALLANCE

Ballance was a split off Eastland—Primitive Friends. The brick building was built in 1846 on the acre given by the Ballance and Smedley families. Each gave one half acre towards the building and grave yard in 1839. It was never under the care of Little Britain Monthly Meeting. The meeting was inactive by the beginning of this century, although the last member died about 1970.In 1749, Penn Hill was established as worship group. On 17 Eighth month1761, Little Britain Preparative Meeting was established. This is the same meeting. Michael King gave Land for the meetinghouse. The present brick meeting house was built in 1823 by Jeremiah Brown to replace a building too small for all to hear his 'minister' wife.

EASTLAND

Eastland, in 1796, asked to hold a meeting of their own. Nottingham Quarterly Meeting granted permission in 1798 for them to continue to hold meetings in the schoolhouse on Henry Reynolds land. The stone building was erected that year for £332, 17 shillings, 6 pence.

Eastland Meeting. *Photo by Gail Pietrzyk.*

The oldest meetinghouse in the area is Eastland. It was built in 1803 after members had met at Henry Reynolds house, behind the present site since 1796.

PENN HILL

Penn Hill was built in 1823, after outgrowing the former houses. Jeremiah Brown, the owner of the local slate quarry, married his third wife, Mercy Shreve. Although she was blind, Jeremiah didn't realize it until he asked her directions in her home territory of New Jersey. He almost didn't marry her with this terrible discovery. She was a 'minister' and traveled among the members that had been read out of meeting and attracted many to hear her.

Penn Hill Meeting. *Photo by Gail Pietrzyk.*

Jeremiah built the brick structure, from bricks made on the Smedley farm, to accommodate the 400 or so members. The bricks were made near a willow patch. The willow was used to make baskets for sale. Unfortunately Mercy died just before the meetinghouse was finished. It is interesting to me that Sandy Spring and Penn Hill, built about the same time look so nearly alike.

LITTLE ELK AND OXFORD

The Oxford area Meetings were established from East Nottingham. Little Elk (1825-1882) and Oxford, which became known as Nottingham Meeting after the former, was laid down. Oxford was established in the home of George Passmore on Pine Street. A lot was bought from John Miller Dickey in 1879 and the meetinghouse was erected for $2,245. The first meeting for worship was held there in September 11, 1879. Early members included Stubbs, Reynolds, Brinton, Way, Kirk, Pugh, Webster, Cope, Thomas and Coates.

A day school was established, which included Negro children. Martha Brown was among the last living alumni.

OCTORARA

A meeting was settled in the valley of the Octorara Creek about midway between West Nottingham and the Conowingo Bridge in 1823. In 1911, Milton T. Garvin rebuilt it in honor of his parents Thomas and Tabitha [Brown] Garvin, who are buried there. He dedicated the grey building on June 9, 1912 as a chapel for the community. Periwinkle and wild plants were what Chalkley Matalck remembered from the spot in the 1930's. The Preston family was a part of this meeting and there were at least 29 members. The meeting was active for about fifty years. The 16'x24'x12' log meeting house was built in 1826.

NOTTINGHAM

Nottingham Meeting, 1901. *Photo from the collection of Edward Plumstead.*

At the Brick Meeting as early as 1702. In 1776 a new meetinghouse was built. Elizabeth P. and George B. Passmore (3 4m 1833-7 9m 1890) were instrumental in starting the meeting in the town of Oxford, PA on Pine Street. It was a joint concern of Nottingham and Penn's Grove Meetings. The Oxford Press ran an article stating that "Rev. J. M. Dickey and Lady of this borough, have recently shown a commendable spirit of liberally donating to the Society of Friends, a lot of land 100 feet on central Avenue, and 300 feet deep, and the selling for $500, an additional 100 feet adjoining to be used for the same purpose. "It was built for $2500. The treasurer was William S. Harlan. Friends arrived by train in June 1879 to dedicate the 40' x 50' building. John Evans, of Oxford, made the 20 benches.

COLORA

Stared in Thomas and Rebecca Warings house before 1841, building built on Warings land for $420. Orthodox or Primitive laid down in 1985. The Lloyd Balderson family held this meeting together for several generations. Lloyd in 1840, at 22, attended Baltimore Yearly Meeting and learned that Griffith Levering lived in the Colora area. Lloyd learned there was a farm for sale for $11 an acre for the worn out tobacco land. In the spring of 1841 Lloyd moved to the Colora. He helped build the meetinghouse on the Waring land that year. The other name associated with this meeting was Joseph Ballance of Little Britain. These joined the Primitive Friends in Baltimore who met at the home of Joseph I. Hopkins. The group was joined by a group at Dunning's Creek, in Bedford County, PA. Eventually a group from Fallsington in Bucks County became the headquarters for the Yearly Meeting, Fishertown joined the Orthodox.

Notes on Contributors

ALICE L. BEARD born 20 October 1948, the daughter of Larry G. and Dolores E. Tucker Baker in Lancaster, Lancaster County, PA. Married 22 December 1967 to Harold W. Beard. Two children. Terry Steven Beard, born 9 March 1969 and Douglas Paul Beard, born 19 December 1974.

Member of the Octorara Chapter Daughters of the American Revolution since 1987 and serve as the Chapter Registrar, being elected in 2001.

Author of *Births, Deaths and Marriages of the Nottingham Quakers, 1680-1889.* "I began researching my family genealogy in 1970 after the birth of my first son. At first genealogy was a hobby, but now it is a passion. Through my research, I found that I descend from five of the original purchasers of the Nottingham Lots: William and James Brown, John Churchman, Joel Baily and Henry Reynolds."

ROBERT W. DAY, born 5 June 1947 in Philadelphia, PA, the son of William Warwick and Mary (Zurn) Day. After graduating from the College of William and Mary (VA), Bob earned a M.Ed. from Georgia State University, Atlanta, and a Ph.D. from Florida State University. Dr. Day's career includes 24 years as a community college administrator, and most recently, Postsecondary Director at the SC School for the Deaf and the Blind in Spartanburg, SC.

Dr. Day is a member of the Historical Society of Pennsylvania and past member of Maryland Genealogical Society.

"I have researched the family since 1976. My grandfather Sidney Cassell Day, Jr. was native of Darlington, Harford County, MD, with deep Quaker roots in Cecil County to early 1700's. Enjoy antiques, foreign travel, local history, and serve on several local boards including the Upstate SC Workforce Investment Board Youth Council."

SUZANNE P. LAMBORN graduated from George School in 1955 and Millersville State Teachers College in 1959. She was continually involved in education for many years by teaching and serving on the Oxford Area School Board. After her husband George chose to stop being a dairy farmer, Sue started researching the many related family lines. She has been clerk of Little Britain Monthly Meeting and involved with the Solanco Historical Society. Her other passion is saving farmland from development, while serving on the Chester County Ag Development Council since 1982.

Index of Settlers and their relations

The following index of names found in the genealogical essay beginning on page 40, is arranged by the names of the first settlers as they appear in the essay. Below the settlers name are listed, in alphabetical order, the names of individuals mentioned in the biographical sketch and in the family trees comprising the section on the settler. Readers interested in locating references to an individual are advised to read through each of the Settlers.

Mary Royal Coles
William Coles
______ Cook
William Cornell
Rachel Cowgale
Sarah Davis
John Davis
Rebekah Davis
John Daye
Lydis (Ross) Daye
Rebekah Daye
John Dutton
Margaret Exton Reynolds
Jacob Haines
Lydia (Johnson) Haines
Mary Haines
Mary (Coles) Haines
Prudence Haines
Sarah Haines
Sarah Haines
William Haines
William Hawkes
Roger Jackson
Mary Job
John Hoopes
Rachel Johns
Jane Jones
Joseph Pyle
James Kenneily
Prudence Lanckford Clayton
______ Moulder
Robert Moulder
Thomas Pearson
John Piggott
Caleb Pusey
Benjamin Reynolds
Catherine ______ Reynolds
Catherine Reynolds
Christian Reynolds
David Reynolds
Deborah Reynolds
Elijah Reynolds
Francis Reynolds
Hannah Reynolds
Henry Reynolds
Henry Reynolds, Jr.
Isaac Reynolds
Jacob Reynolds
Jeremiah Reynolds
Jesse Reynolds
John Reynolds
Jonathan Reynolds
Joseph Reynolds
Lydia Reynolds
Margaret Reynolds
Margaret Exton Reynolds
Martha ______ Reynolds
Mary Reynolds
Prudence Reynolds
Rachel Reynolds
Samuel Reynolds
Thomas Reynolds
William Reynolds
Ann Rich
Wooly Rosen
Mary Royal
James Sandelands
Isaac Sharp
Susanna Sidwell
Richard Sidwell
Joseph Talbot
Joseph Townsend
Phebe White
Ann Worley

JOHN RICHARDSON

Joel Baily
Cornelius Empson
Richard Halliwell
Thomas Hollingsworth
John Husey
Howell James
Alphonusus Kirk

Thomas Pierson
Caleb Pusey
Robert Pyle
John Richardson
Philip Roman
Isaac Taylor
CORNELIUS EMPSON
EBENEZER EMPSON
Mary Block
Thomas Conoway
Morgan Durett
Ann Empson
Charles Empson
Cornelius Empson
Ebenezer Empson
Elizabeth Empson
James Empson
Jonathan Empson
Mary Empson
Mary (Clark) Empson
Rebecca Empson
Richard Empson
Sarah Empson
Susannah Empson
William Empson
_____ Salif
Erasmus Stidham
Valentine Hollingsworth
Barbara Maislander
Valentine Morgan
Mary Richardson
Elizabeth Sanderson
Mary Sanderson
Adam Sharpley
Christian Stalcap
William Stockdale
John Taylor
Martha Taylor
Robert Wilson
Sarah Wilson
Joseph Wood
Susannah Wood
JOEL BAILY
Anne Baily
Daniel Baily (Bayly)
Daniel Baily
Isaac Baily
Joel Baily
John Baily
Josiah Baily
Mary Baily
Mary _____ Baily (Bayly)
Mary Baily Stewart
Mary Baily Harlan
Thomas Baily
Sarah Bentley
Betty Caldwell
Francis Chadsey
Jeremiah Cloud
James Craft
Thomas Dutton
Dinah Harlan
Ezekiel Harlan
George Harlan
Hannah Harlan
Joel Harlan
John Harlan
Michael Harlan
Rebecca Harlan
Susanna Harlan
Hugh Harris
Olive Harris
Isaac Ingram
Miriam Ingram
Abigail Johnson
Robert Johnson
Henry Marsh
Mary Marsh
Sarah Marsh
Henry Nayle
William Penn
Lydia Pusey

William Pusey
John Radley
Martha Richardson
_____ Short
Ann Short
Miriam Short
William Smith
Alexander Stewart
Ann Stewart
Jane Stewart
Mary Stewart
Robert Stewart
Joseph Taylor
Josiah Taylor
George Thompson
JAMES COOPER
John Ball
John Blunston
John Clark
Thomas Collier
Calvin Cooper
George Cooper
Hannah Cooper
Hannah _____ Cooper
James Cooper
John Cooper
Mary Cooper
Phebe Cooper
Sarah Cooper
William Cooper
Francis Crompton
John Dixon
Thomas Dixon
Anna Elizabeth Hall
Henry Giles
Phebe Hall
Samuel Hall
Daniel Hybert
Elizabeth Jeffries
James Johnson
Jno. Kirk
Mary Ludwedge
John Marshall
Margaret Miller
Mary Miller
Samuel Miller
Rachel Moore
Rebecca Moore
James Philips
Catherine Powell
Elizabeth Pyle
John Roads
Robert Scothorn
Robert Smith
Susanna Truman
JAMES BROWN
Joel Baily
Esther (Hester) Baker
Henry Baker
Margaret (Hardman) Baker
Edward Beason
Rachel Beeson
Joseph Besse
Abigail Brown
Catherine Brown
Clayton Brown
Daniel Brown
Ebenezer Brown
Elizabeth Brown
Esther Brown
Hannah Brown
Isaac Brown
Jacob Brown
James Brown
Jeremiah Brown
John Brown
Joseph Brown
Judith Brown
Margaret Brown
Margery Brown
Mary Brown
Mary _____ Brown

Mercer Brown
Patience Brown
Rachel Brown
Richard Brown
Samuel Brown
Thomas Brown
Timothy Brown
William Brown
Dinah Churchman
Hannah (Seary) Churchman
John Churchman
Miriam Churchman
Susanna Churchman
William Churchman
Honor Clayton
Prudence Clayton
Prudence (Lanckford) Clayton
William Clayton
William Coles
______ Collett
James Cooper
Elizabeth Cowgill
Ellin Cowgill
John Cowgill
______ Crompton
Joseph Elgar
Mary Elgar
Susanna Elgar
Cornelius Empson
Elisha Gatchell
Hannah Gatchell
Sarah (Churchman) Gatchell
Miriam Gregg
______ Haines
Elizabeth Harris
William Harris
Daniel Job
Mary Jones
Abigail (Sharpley) Kirk
Alphonsus Kirk
Elizabeth Kirk
Elizabeth Knight
William Knight
Mary Matthews
Ann Mercer
Mary Mercer
Thomas Mercer
Edward Norton
Mary Norton
Susanna Oldham
Abigail Piggott
Benjamin Piggott
Elizabeth Piggott
James Piggott
Jeremiah Piggott
Jeremiah Piggott (2)
John Piggott
Margery Piggott
Margery Piggott (2)
Samuel Piggott
Susannah Piggott
William Piggott
Dorothy Presland
Woole Rawson
Hannah Reynolds
Henry Reynolds
William Reynolds
Jane Richards
John Richardson
Mary Robbins
Thomas Rogers
Mary Royal
Hannah Seary
Margaret Sinkler
George Slater
Lydia Slater
Sarah Slater
Joseph Trimble
Catherine Williams
Robert Williams
Anna Wilson
Mary Winter

RANDALL JANNEY

Richard Hill
Randall Janney
Thomas Janney
William Janney
Frances Righton
Sarah Righton
William Righton
Deborah Webb
Jno. Willmer

JOHN CHURCHMAN

Abigail Brown
Ann (Mercer) Brown
Daniel Brown
David Brown
Dinah Brown
Elizabeth (Kirk) Brown
Esther (Baker-Yearsley) Brown
Esther (Yearsley) Brown
Hannah (Gatchell) Brown
Isaiah Brown
James Brown
John Brown
Joshua Brown
Margaret Brown
Messer Brown
Sarah Brown
William Brown
Abigail Churchman
David Churchman
Deborah Churchman
Dinah Churchman
Edward Churchman
Elijah Churchman
Elizabeth (Leader) Churchman
Enoch Churchman
George Churchman
Hannah Churchman
John Churchman
Miriam Churchman
Robert Churchman
Sarah Churchman
Susanna Churchman
Thomas Churchman
William Churchman
David Gatchell
Joseph Gatchell
Gainor James
Hannah James
Mordecai James
Katherine Jones
Ann Knight
David Parry
Elizabeth (Ely) Parry
Rowland Parry
Jane Pugh
Katherine Reynolds
Hannah Seary
Sarah Seary
Thomas Seary
Jane Taylor
Joseph Trimble
Mary Trimble
William Trimble

ROBERT DUTTON

Joel Baily
John Baldwin
Ann Brown
Ann (Mercer) Brown
William Brown
Thomas Cartwright
Mary Darlington
Ann Dutton
Edward Dutton
Elizabeth Dutton
John Dutton
Mary Dutton
Robert Dutton
Thomas Dutton
Joseph England
Lewis England
John Nield

Robert Taylor
John White
SAMUEL LITTLER
Josiah Ballinger
Thomas Barrett
Elisha Brown
Morgan Bryan
E. Gatchell
Alice Littler
John Littler
Joshua Littler
Mary Littler
Minshall Littler
Nathan Littler
Rachel Littler
Samuel Littler
Sarah Littler
Susannah Littler
Thomas Littler
William Littler
John Minshall
Rachel Minshall
Deborah Oldham
Susannah (Few) Oldham
Thomas Oldham
Jane Pugh
John Pugh
Joshua Pugh
Caleb Pusey
Alexander Ross
Katherine (Chambers) Ross
Mary Ross
Simon Taylor
Thomas Taylor
Evan Thomas
Marius Trent
Lydia Woodward
James Wright
ANDREW JOB(E)
Thomas Brassey
Elizabeth (Harris) Brown
Mary Brown
Samuel Brown
George Churchman
Daniel Defoe
Abigail Gatchell
Elisha Gatchell
Rachel (Wilcox) Gatchell
Sarah Gatchell
Abraham Job
Benjamin Job
Caleb Job
Daniel Job
Daniel Defoe Job
Enoch (1) Job
Enoch (2) Job
Hannah Job
Jacob Job
James Job
Joshua Job
Mary Job
Patience Job
Thomas Job
Andrew Job(e)
Elizabeth Maxwell
Margaret McCoy
Robert McCoy
Jane Pugh
John Pugh
Sarah Pugh
William Pusey
Joseph Trimble
Elizabeth Vernon
Thomas Vernon
John White
Mary White
Samuel White
William White
JOHN BEALS
Josiah Ballengar
Elizabeth Beals
Jacob Beals

John Beals
Lydia Beals
  Mary Beals
  Mary Beals
  Patience Beals
  Sarah Beals
  Thomas Beals
  William Beals
  Sarah Bowater
  Sarah (Edge) Bowater
  Thomas Bowater
  John Brooksby
  Mary Brooksby
  John Chambers
  Rebeckah Chambers
  Mary Clayton
  Prudence (Lanckford) Clayton
  William Clayton
  Mary Davis
  Richard Harrold
  Charity Jones
  John Jones
  Judith Jones
  Mary Jones
  Sarah Jones
  Joseph Jones
  John Mills
  Jonathan Mills
  Mary (1) Mills
  Mary (2) Mills
  Rachel Mills
Richard Mills
Thomas Mills

Joel Baily
Arthur Barrett
Deborah Barrett
Hannah Barrett
John Barrett
Joseph Barrett
Lydia Barrett
Mary Barrett
Rachel Barrett
Rebekah Barrett
Richard Barrett
Susanna Barrett
Thomas Barrett
William Barrett
Anne Brown
Ellen Brown
Esther Brown
Hannah Brown
Hannah (Gatchell) Brown
Jane (Richards) Brown
Jeremiah Brown
Joshua Brown
Mary Brown
Mary (Cole) Brown
Mercer (Messer) Brown
Thomas Brown
Lydia Chambers
  Abel Chandlee
  Benjamin Chandlee
  Cottey Chandlee
  Ellis Chandlee
  Goldsmith Chandlee
  Hannah Chandlee
  Isaac Chandlee
  Joanna Chandlee
  John Chandlee
  Mary Chandlee
  Sarah Chandlee
  William Chandlee
  Aaron Coppock
  Ann Coppock
  John Coppock
  Joseph Coppock
  Lydia Coppock
  Margaret Coppock
  Martha Coppock
  Mary Coppock
  Miriam Coppock

Samuel Coppock
Sarah Coppock
Thomas Coppock
Abel Cottey
Mary Cottey
Sarah Cottey
Joseph Coulson
Margaret Coulson
Joseph Elgar
Mary Elgar
Edward Folwell
Mary Folwell
_____ Frazer
Sarah Frazer
Anne _____ Gatchell
Abigail Gatchell
Elisha Gatchell
Elizabeth Gatchell
Elizabeth (Boude) Gatchell
Hannah Gatchell
Jeremiah Gatchell
Sarah Gatchell
Elizabeth Giles Oldham
Elizabeth Goulding
Catherine Hagan
Margaret Hagan
Charity Harris
John Harris
Phebe Harris
Ann Hayes
Thomas Hughes
Abraham Job
Ann Job
Elizabeth (Vernon) Job
Enoch Job
Mary Job
Thomas Job
Richard Jones
Hannah King
Isabel (Pennell) King
James King
Jane King
Margaret King
Mary King
Michael King
Thomas King
Vincent King
Abner Kirk
Elizabeth (Richards) Kirk
Roger Kirk
Timothy Kirk
Daniel Maule
Thomas Maule
Zillah Maule
Elizabeth Maxwell
Neal McCaskey
James Midcalf
Margaret Midcalf
Rachel Midcalf
Edward Mitchell
Hannah Oldham
Thomas Oldham
Isabel Pennell
Hannah Piggott
John Price
Mary Pugh
_____ Robinson
Martha Robinson
Eunice Rogers
Jeremiah Sergent
_____ Sheperd
Miriam Short
Abraham Sidwell
Ann Sidwell
Anne Sidwell
Frances (West) Sidwell
Henry Sidwell
Hugh Sidwell
Isaac Sidwell
Jacob Sidwell
John Sidwell
Joseph Sidwell

Mary Sidwell
Richard Sidwell
______ Sinclair
Mary Sinclair
George Thompson
Ralph Thompson
Ann White
Elizabeth White
John White
Samuel White
William White
Barnabas Wilcox
Rachel Wilcox
Sarah Wilcox
Benjamin Wilson
Anne (Stone) Worley
Henry Worley
Mary Worley
Hannah Yarnall

Made in United States
Orlando, FL
26 February 2023

30447446R00059